# EASY-CARE
# ROSES

## LOW-MAINTENANCE
## CHARMERS

Stephen Scanniello

Guest Editor

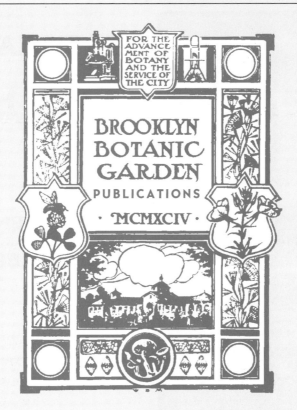

**FOR THE ADVANCE MENT OF BOTANY AND THE SERVICE OF THE CITY**

**BROOKLYN BOTANIC GARDEN PUBLICATIONS · MCMXCIV ·**

**Janet Marinelli**
SERIES EDITOR

**Anne Witte Garland**
ASSOCIATE EDITOR

**Bekka Lindstrom**
ART DIRECTOR

**Stephen K.M. Tim**
VICE PRESIDENT, SCIENCE & PUBLICATIONS

**Judith D. Zuk**
PRESIDENT

**Elizabeth Scholtz**
DIRECTOR EMERITUS

Handbook #142

Copyright © Spring 1995 by the Brooklyn Botanic Garden, Inc.

BBG gardening handbooks are published quarterly at 1000 Washington Ave., Brooklyn, NY 11225

Subscription included in Brooklyn Botanic Garden membership dues ($25.00 per year)

ISSN 0362-5850 ISBN # 0-945352-87-5

PRINTED IN KOREA

Cover photograph: 'Thérèse Bugnet'

# Table of Contents

# A NEW LOOK AT ROSES

### BY STEPHEN SCANNIELLO

**H**AVE YOU EVER tried to grow a rose, only to watch it languish from disease or insect infestation, and eventually die?

The photos in catalogs, books and nursery advertisements are picture-perfect. But when you bring the roses home to your garden, the trouble begins.

This complaint is heard from gardeners across the country. Somehow, that spectacular hybrid tea from the mail-order catalog just doesn't live up to its promise when it's actually growing in your mountaintop garden. And after all is said and done, you'll probably need to go out next spring and buy new plants, since they never seem to survive your winters.

On the other hand, if you're a gardener in the deep South, you may wonder why your roses quickly become a living textbook of rose problems, despite the milder winters.

Traditionally, roses have been coddled, treated as the fussiest of garden plants. When I first started growing roses, spraying for insects and diseases was a regular part of the routine. In the last ten years, however, there has been a strong movement away from this school of thought. Thanks to the efforts of plant preservation groups such as the Heritage Rose Foundation, the general public is becoming increasingly aware of entire classes of roses that are easier to grow and don't require a constant onslaught of harsh chemicals to fend off insects and diseases.

Are there roses that can survive without spraying? Any that can withstand the cold winters of zone 3? That thrive where there isn't a cold winter dormant period? Can you grow roses in containers? Can you grow your grandmother's roses from cuttings? An answer to each of these questions can be found in the following pages. And, by the way, the answer is yes.

A new generation of rosarians from all over the country has contributed to this book. Gardeners from large public gardens, nursery professionals, hybridizers and homeowners all offer their personal insights on growing roses—from

Roses don't need to be coddled—or doused with chemicals—to thrive. Here, 'Belinda' provides a profusion of pink blossoms.

practical tips on pruning roses and landscaping with roses to a detailed section on chemical-free rose care.

Even if you follow all the recommended horticultural techniques, you may have problems if you choose the wrong rose for your garden. There *is* a rose for every garden. But not every rose is ideal for every garden. In this volume, rosarians from diverse climates—from southern Texas to the mountaintops of Vermont—recommend their favorite and easiest-to-grow roses. From miniature roses to vigorous climbers, old roses and some of the newest cultivars are recommended for each region.

You'll also learn how to search for roses in cemeteries, old homesteads, even long-forgotten gardens of the inner city—roses that have flourished for decades without any human care at all—and how to propagate these sturdy old rose varieties from cuttings. Finally, you'll get a glimpse of new trends that will shape the future of roses, both here and abroad, for years to come.

All of this was put together with a single object in mind—to enable you to successfully grow beautiful roses that do not need to be sprayed, primped or pampered to survive.

# CLASSIFYING ROSES

BY STEPHEN SCANNIELLO

**F**IFTEEN YEARS AGO we were content to group roses into the following seven categories: hybrid teas, floribundas, grandifloras, miniature roses, climbers, old-fashioned roses and shrub roses (which included anything that didn't fit into one of the other categories). Gardeners today, inspired by the escapades of the rose rustlers, the Heritage Rose Foundation and the many new rose nurseries specializing in unique roses, have been expanding their horizons, and the number of categories has expanded as well.

One general rule to remember is that a modern rose is a rose that belongs to a classification (such as hybrid tea or floribunda) that has evolved from 1867 on. That is the universally accepted date of the first hybrid tea rose. Old garden roses (also known as antique roses, old-fashioned roses, old roses, even "grandma's roses") are roses that belong to a classification that existed before 1867.

## THE BASIC ROSE-CLASSIFICATION SYSTEM

OLD GARDEN ROSES—15 CLASSES:

🌹 **Species**—The wild roses—the source of all other rose varieties. Producing simple, very fragrant flowers once a year in spring, they're carefree, disease resistant and hardy.

🌹 **Gallicas**—Descendants of *R. gallica*, probably the oldest cultivated rose in existence in the West. These are low shrubs, suckering (producing new shoots along the roots), with large, fragrant flowers borne singly or in clusters.

🌹 **Damasks**—Closely related to gallicas but larger and taller, damasks are the

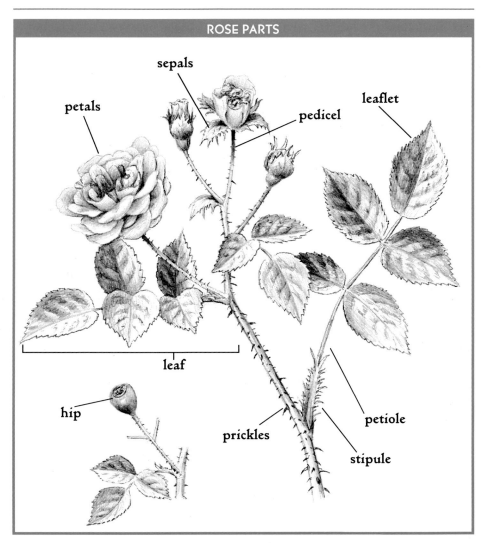

**ROSE PARTS**

Knowing the various parts of a rose—whether a modern or old-garden specimen—can help you distinguish one variety from another.

most fragrant of the old garden roses, with semi-double or double blooms. 'Autumn Damask' is the only repeat bloomer.

**Albas**—Believed to be crosses between damask or gallica roses and *R. canina,* the albas are upright, tall and vigorous, with sparse prickles, tough leaves and mostly fully double blooms.

◉ **Centifolias**—Known as cabbage roses for their globe-like flowers. Centifolias may be a cross between 'Autumn Damask' and an alba. They're taller than gallicas, with drooping leaves, prickly stems and fragrant, nodding flowers.

◉ **Moss roses**—"Sported" (genetically mutated) from centifolias or damasks, moss roses have drooping foliage and sepals, hips and flower stalks covered with mossy growth that gives off a pine or resin scent when rubbed.

◉ **Chinas**—Everblooming roses first discovered in China. Brought in the late 18th century to Europe, where many new cultivars were created. These are the everblooming ancestors of all modern, repeat-blooming roses. Some Chinas are low growing; some have tall canes and can be treated as climbers. Their small flowers usually change from light to dark; they're borne on short stems and have a distinct, light fragrance.

◉ **Teas**—Very fragrant forms of the China class, with dainty leaves and stems. The first teas were crosses between *R. chinensis* and *R. gigantea*.

◉ **Noisettes**—The original Noisettes were a cross between a China rose and European rose, and are not very hardy.

◉ **Bourbons**—The original Bourbon was an accidental hybrid of Chinas and 'Autumn Damask', a repeat bloomer with larger, fragrant flowers.

◉ **Hybrid Chinas**—First generation of crosses between Chinas and other rose varieties, developed for larger flowers.

◉ **Hybrid Bourbons**—First generation of crosses between the original Bourbons and gallicas or damask hybrids, these have various flower colors and growth habits.

◉ **Hybrid Noisettes**—First generation of crosses between Noisettes and Bourbons, Chinas and tea roses, with larger flowers.

◉ **Portlands**—Popular in the early 19th century because of their repeat-blooming flowers.

◉ **Hybrid perpetuals**—Hybrids of Portland roses, hybrid Chinas, gallicas and

'QUATRE SAISONS BLANC' (A Moss)

'PENELOPE' (A Hybrid Musk)

'FASHION' (A Floribunda)

'DAINTY BESS' (A Hybrid Tea)

Bourbons, these were very popular in the 19th century. They're very hardy, ranging from sprawling to upright in habit, with fragrant, many-petaled flowers on short stems.

**MODERN ROSES—10 CLASSES:**

**Hybrid teas**—Very popular modern roses with large flowers on long stems. Hybrid teas bloom often, in a wide range of colors; many are fragrant.

🌹 **Polyanthas**—Low-growing shrubs with large clusters of small flowers ("polyantha" means "many-flowered"). They grow to about 2 feet, are extremely hardy and bloom continuously, though generally with little fragrance.

🌹 **Floribundas**—Originally hybrids between polyanthas and hybrid teas. Floribundas (the name means "cluster-flowered") are hardy, large, shrubby bushes that bloom continuously all summer.

🌹 **Grandifloras**—Originally crosses between hybrid teas and floribundas, with clustered flowers like the floribundas but larger, and with the long stems of hybrid teas. Grandifloras are tall, often over 6 feet, with masses of color.

🌹 **Miniatures**—Except for the miniature cascading and climbing roses, these grow to just 10 to 18 inches, with proportionately small leaves, stems and flowers. They're very hardy, and unlike many modern roses, most grow on their own rootstocks.

🌹 **Climbing roses**—No roses have tendrils or other means for climbing on their own, but the climbers have tall canes that with support can be trained to grow upright. Some are everblooming; others bloom just once at the beginning of the season. Ramblers are climbing roses with very pliable canes.

🌹 **Shrub roses**—A catch-all category including robust, spreading roses that bloom fairly constantly, some with single flowers, others double.

🌹 **Hybrid musks**—Shrub roses only distantly related to the musk rose. Can tolerate poor growing conditions, such as poor soil and shade. Many set good hips (fruits). Some hybrid musks can be trained as climbers.

🌹 **Eglantine hybrids**—Crosses between the species eglantine rose and hybrid perpetuals, Bourbons or other roses, these are large, arching shrubs that can reach 10 to 12 feet. They produce early leaves with a spicy apple scent, fragrant blooms borne either singly or in clusters and bright-red hips in autumn.

🌹 **Rugosa hybrids**—Hybrids of hybrid teas and *R. rugosa*. Some of the hardiest roses, these are very easy-care, disease-resistant roses.

# OLD ROSES

**Long-forgotten shrubs
that have withstood decades of
blackspot and mildew, aphid and beetle attacks,
freezes and droughts—
without any of the chemical weapons
in the modern rosarian's arsenal**

## Finding Old Roses

### BY RUTH KNOPF

TRADD STREET YELLOW"..."German Cemetery Rose"..."The Sport"..."Cathryn's Bouquet"..."The Heart-Petal Rose." These are all roses growing in my garden. These aren't their official names, but rather descriptive ones that remind me where I found them. Learning their proper names will

Above: "The Heart-Petal Rose" is found in many old gardens in South Carolina.

"Tradd St. Yellow". A climbing tea that turns a butter yellow as it matures, it is named after the street where it was found growing.

come with time, if at all. To me what is important is not the names, but the fact that these local roses are a part not only of our garden history but of our lives. Finding them creates a tie that binds them to your heart.

When I discovered old roses in 1976, there were few sources for buying them. Old roses were out of style, and nurseries usually offer only what is in demand. So in order to have roses I admired, I learned to root them and thus began my collecting. Whenever someone told me of a rose that had been in their family or was growing in an old garden, I went to see it and often returned with cuttings to try.

After a while I found myself looking for roses wherever I go. To be prepared, I take plastic bags and clippers in my car. I look for old roses in yards of older houses, cemeteries and vacant lots. I've become brave and have learned to knock on doors and explain my mission. At first the owner looks at you with suspicion, but when you finally see a smile, you know you've gotten the preservation message across and have secured a future for the rose. I always try to get as much history as possible about the rose and to photograph the plant and its location.

In the beginning, I collected anything that didn't look like a hybrid tea bush, and usually it was an old rose. After a while, your eye becomes trained to recognize the different forms various classes of roses take. You also learn to look for the way the leaves are shaped and grow, and you often have to do this from a distance. For example, although tea roses vary, they usually have an upright but graceful, spreading growth habit. The leaves are smooth though not shiny, and can be longer than average. If you can see this from the car, you know it calls for a closer look.

Identification is a controversial subject among some old-rose collectors and growers. Rose research is hard work and can often be a slow process. But it's rewarding, too—like unraveling a mystery. Still, the roses will be blooming in our gardens regardless of what we call them. And even if we eventually find our roses' official titles, I hope they will always keep their own special names—like "Tradd Street Yellow," "German Cemetery Rose," "Cathryn's Bouquet," and "The Heart-Petal Rose."

# Cemetery Roses Live On

## BY TERI TILLMAN

ROSES AND CEMETERIES have a centuries-long association, dating back to the earliest days of Christianity, when roses were carved on the tombstones of martyrs as a symbol of the Resurrection and divine mercy. While delicately carved roses can still be seen on an occasional headstone, the most beautiful roses found at cemeteries today are those planted long ago by unknown hands. Old cemeteries have become valuable repositories of long-forgotten antique rose varieties. With little or no care, these hardy shrubs have withstood decades of blackspot and mildew, aphid and beetle attacks, freezes and drought. And they've withstood all these onslaughts without the benefit of any of the chemical weapons usually found in the modern rosarian's arsenal.

A few minutes from my home in historic downtown Natchez, Mississippi, lies just such a cemetery full of old garden roses—some of which are believed to be more than a hundred years old. Established in 1824, the Natchez City Cemetery consists of more than 90 acres of gently rolling land overlooking the steep bluffs of the Mississippi River. Outstanding marble monuments and exquisitely detailed cast-iron fences have earned it a place on the National Register of Historic Places. Its varied collection of old garden roses, including species roses, chinas, teas, Noisettes, Bourbons and polyanthas, has attracted the attention of old-rose fanciers from around the country.

Protecting this collection of heritage roses has become a project for a few volunteers from the local Garden Club of America, who have embarked on an ambitious

A Noisette thrives at a grave site.
Old cemeteries have become valuable
repositories of long-forgotten rose
varieties.

program to prune and protect all the surviving cemetery roses. Although these horticultural treasures have survived decades of neglect, in recent years new enemies have appeared that threaten to render cemetery roses extinct: humans and their machines. One misdirected swing of a weedeater or one careless pass of a riding mower can wipe out decades of growth and horticultural history.

A scraggly specimen of 'Old Blush' a few feet from Rosalie Beekman's grave was the target of our initial efforts. Seven-year-old Rosalie earned her place in Natchez history when she became the only casualty of a naval bombardment in Natchez-Under-the-Hill in 1863. Today Rosalie's rosebush is once again thriving, thanks to a double layer of weedcloth and a 4-foot square, 2-inch thick layer of pine bark mulch. Straight lines, square corners and generous amounts of mulch (plus an upside-down tomato cage over new plants) seem to be the key to keeping the weedeaters at bay.

With the permission of the cemetery board, we have also undertaken a limited propagation program, focusing on those roses whose identities are unknown ("mystery" roses), or those whose long-term survival is in jeopardy, such as a 'Marie Pavié' growing in the shade of a large pecan tree. One mystery rose at the cemetery, believed to be the same as "Spice," a mystery rose from Bermuda, has been propagated and planted at the grave of a young woman known only as Louise. Many years ago Louise came up to Natchez from New Orleans to marry a local man. When the marriage plans fell through, Louise resorted to earning her living as a prostitute and succumbed to an unknown illness. She would have been buried in a pauper's grave but for the sympathy of a local minister who paid

Although cemetery roses like 'Safrano' have survived decades of neglect, they are now threatened with extinction by weedeaters and riding mowers.

for her burial. Today, a mystery rose marks the grave of this mystery woman whose headstone reads simply, "Louise the Unfortunate."

Last year the Heritage Rose Foundation initiated another phase of our preservation program when it planted ten heritage roses at the cemetery to replace some of those lost over the years. One of these grows next to Florence Irene Ford's grave. Only ten years old when she died, Florence had always been terribly afraid of thunderstorms. Her parents, frantic with worry about their daughter even after her death, devised a way to keep her company during stormy weather. Behind her headstone a heavy metal door opens up to a flight of steps that descend 6 feet into the earth. The steps terminate abruptly at a solid (once transparent) wall. Every stormy night for as long as they lived, Florence's parents rode out to the cemetery, climbed down the steps and sat out the storm with their daughter. Today an 'Archduke Charles' commemorates Florence's untimely death and her parents' devotion.

Natchez, perhaps more than most old southern towns, has worked hard to preserve its historical identity. Although the efforts have focused so far primarily on the city's architecture, I believe that future conservation efforts will expand to include our horticultural heritage. Many of the glorious gardens of Natchez have vanished without a trace, but a hint of their beauty remains in the collection of antique roses at the City Cemetery. By protecting, propagating and replacing the old roses at the graveyard, we hope to perpetuate the ancient tradition of tombs adorned with roses while preserving a unique part of our community's horticultural history.

# PROPAGATING ROSES FROM CUTTINGS

## BY MALCOLM M. MANNERS

ONCE YOU'VE TAKEN cuttings of old roses from a cemetery, old house or vacant lot, what's the next step? Most roses are easily propagated by rooting cuttings. Here are some tips for success:

🌹 **Age**—Make sure you take cuttings from firm but young stems. On a repeat-flowering variety, that would be stems on which the flowers are fading or from which the petals have just fallen. On a once-flowering plant, you can use stems from which the flowers are fading in the spring, or similar-age wood from subsequent growth flushes throughout the summer or fall.

🌹 **Leaves**—Roses root best if the cutting has some leaves still attached, to provide sugars from photosynthesis as well as root-promoting hormones. Some varieties will root from leafless cuttings, but it's better to allow two or three leaves to remain. Keep a spray bottle of water handy to mist over the cuttings while working on them, to keep them crisp, since wilted cuttings often fail to root.

🌹 **Cuts and "wounding"**—Roses can form roots at any point along the stem, so the exact site of the cut is not important. Many people "wound" the base of the cutting, either by making 1/2- to 1-inch vertical slits through the bark, or by slicing a strip of bark off one or two sides of the base of the cutting with the clipper blade. Difficult varieties often benefit from such wounding, sending out roots all along the wound.

🌹 **Rooting hormones**—You can root most rose varieties without the use of hormone preparations. This is because rose cuttings contain auxin (indoleacetic acid—"IAA"), a natural root-promoting hormone. It is produced by the leaves and growing buds or shoot tips and accumulates at the bottom of a cutting, where the roots will form. But some roses apparently don't produce adequate supplies of auxin and are difficult to root. If they produce any roots at all, they are few and weak. So, many growers apply a commercial hormone preparation to stimulate the production of strong roots. These

Take cuttings from firm, young stems with leaves. Make the cut at a 45° angle.

**Create a small tent with a plastic bag or jar to maintain high humidity around cuttings.**

products all contain synthetic auxin, usually indolebutyric acid (IBA) and/or naphthaleneacetic acid (NAA).

**Moisture**—One of the most important factors in successfully rooting cuttings is maintaining adequate moisture, both in the soil and in the form of humidity in the air. Place the cuttings in pots of moist sand or potting soil, then cover them with a plastic bag, mayonnaise jar or inverted two-liter soft drink bottle with the top cut off, creating a small tent or "greenhouse" to maintain high humidity around the cuttings.

**Light**—Roses root best in bright light. But when using the mini-greenhouse method, it's important to avoid overheating by giving some shade from hot, midday sun. Put the cuttings in bright shade, such as against the north wall of a building or under a tree, to allow rooting without too much heat build-up.

**Season**—Most cuttings root best in the spring or early summer, when the weather is warm but not miserably hot. You can root cuttings at other times of the year, but it may take longer and a smaller percentage of them may take. A few types (such as the gallicas) may root more successfully in the autumn.

**Timing**—In May or early June, some varieties will have good roots in as little as two weeks. Nearly any variety can be rooted in three to four weeks at that time of year. At other times the process takes longer—up to seven or eight weeks. There are several ways to tell whether a cutting is rooted. You can tug lightly on it, and if it resists being pulled out of the pot, it likely has roots. Also, roots growing out the drainage holes in the bottom of the pot are a sure indication of success. Cuttings that are actively growing new leaves usually have roots, whereas unrooted cuttings tend not to produce much new top growth.

Once the cuttings are rooted and have been removed from the rooting area, harden them off for a few days by putting the pots in a cool, shady area. Moving them immediately into hot sunshine may damage or even kill the plants. Once they have a good, large root system and are putting out new growth, they can be moved into brighter light.

# A Mystery Rose

BY CHARLES A. WALKER, JR.

THE MYSTERY ROSE. No, it isn't a horticultural character from a detective novel—just a rose whose original name has been lost. It turned up in an out-of-the-way place, along a rural roadside, but it could as easily have been passed down in several generations of a family or encountered in an old cemetery, struggling to survive the weedeater. I root a cutting from it, and as it begins growing in my garden, my appreciation for it grows as well. I don't really need to know this mystery rose's original identity in order to completely enjoy its beauty and fragrance—but human curiosity eventually gets the best of me, and off I go on a quest for its true name.

Since blooms are the most eye-catching feature of roses, I begin by comparing the flowers of my foundling with labeled roses in gardens or with photographs in books. After a while it becomes evident that my rose isn't in the gardens I'm visiting. The photographs aren't much help either; the colors don't seem to match, or the blooms are too far in the background to be useful.

So I show my mystery rose to some heritage-rose experts. One tells me that it might be so-and-so, but he isn't sure. Another says that the first expert was wrong and that it is certainly such-and-such. Someone else ventures a third guess. My experts don't explain how they've reached their conclusions, and when I ask them, I get obscure answers peppered with unfamiliar terms like "Boursault" and "hybrid China," and references to descriptions and illustrations in some books from the 1800s. I come away more puzzled than before.

Luckily I meet some fellow amateur heritage rose enthusiasts. They aren't botanists, but they've learned a half-dozen convenient botanical terms. Before long I'm getting acquainted with parts of a rose plant that I never noticed before: The stipules, for instance, are the pair of little green ribbons that grow at the base of the leaf where it attaches to the stem. These don't seem to be of much use to the plant, but they are very handy in distinguishing roses from each other. The edges of the stipules might be smooth or notched or deeply fringed. Sepals are the five green triangular pieces that enclose the flower petals still in the bud. Their edges can also vary from rose to rose. I learn that prickles (which I had been calling thorns) have different shapes and jut out from the stems at different angles.

"Spice" was discovered and named by old-rose enthusiasts in Bermuda.

Learning these few new terms and paying closer attention to the details in the leaves boosts my confidence in comparing roses, even when they aren't in bloom.

Next, I get a chance to examine several of the books from the 1800s that the experts told me about. There are hundreds of roses described in them, so at first I'm excited about the prospect of discovering the name of my mystery rose among them. But gradually I realize that the descriptions in the books are too sketchy, or too vague, to be of use.

So what do I do with my mystery rose? I keep it, without its original name, and share it with my friends. Maybe I'll give it a new name—something inspired by the place where I found it, the person who first told me about it, or what it looks like growing in my garden. After all, the Bermuda Rose Society has been naming roses this way for more than 40 years, and some of the American nurseries that specialize in old roses have followed suit, even giving mystery roses particular emphasis in their catalogs.

But what if the same mystery rose is found in two different places and inadvertently given two different new names? This need not create a problem. Plant parts or, if necessary, sophisticated biochemical tests could be used to verify that these two roses are really just one. Then one of the new names could be designated as a synonym, just as modern roses often have several synonyms, depending on the countries where they're marketed.

Long snubbed simply because of their missing names, mystery roses are becoming increasingly popular as garden-worthy subjects. By working cooperatively, we can find practical ways to give them confusion-free new names and ensure their continued cultivation and enjoyment for many years to come.

# SPECIES ROSES

## Low-maintenance Charmers

### BY KARLTON HOLMES

HEN I WAS first assigned to work in the Arnold Arboretum's rose garden, I thought, "Karl, you're in trouble now." I began to read about rose care (*just* to brush up, mind you), and I came across material that would have been the envy of the great alchemists of the Middle Ages, including images of blackspot, crown gall, powdery mildew and fire blight. It seemed rose care had a mystique that would confound me at every turn.

That was ages ago now. What had seemed an impossible task is actually a fairly simple one because I found myself in charge of a rose garden that specializes as a collection of species roses—plants that had originally been wild and then were transplanted into a garden setting. With few exceptions, no plants are easier to tend than those that have evolved in the wild; they take care of themselves.

Species roses are the simplest and purest form of roses—essentially the living ancestors of all other roses. It is through breeding, cross-breeding and other genetic manipulation that we have come by the fancier rose forms that are prevalent at flower shops and in many gardens.

## WHAT TO LOOK FOR IN SPECIES ROSES

Like their hybrid progeny, species roses come in a variety of flower colors, from the subtlest and most creamy orange to the sexiest of bordello pinks. There are the whites in *Rosa rugosa alba*, the yellows in *Rosa primula* and *Rosa ecae* and, of course, the pinks and near-reds that dominate the spectrum of species roses. But, much more than color, what sets a species rose apart is the actual form of the flower. Bearing little or no resemblance to their long-stem hybrid counterparts sold on Valentine's Day, species roses have simple, unpretentious flowers—generally five petals open wide, borne singly or in clusters. But even though the form of the flower is less complex than that of many hybrids, the species rose offers year-round interest that many of the hybrids cannot.

*Rosa setigera.* Unlike hybrid roses, species roses have simple flowers, generally with five wide-open petals.

In choosing a species rose, first I'll want a good flower whose color matches the overall scheme that I want to develop. After that, though, I begin to look for other qualities, such as foliage color, texture, scent, fruit (the rose hips) and overall branching pattern. (You'll know you're a true gardener when you become obsessed with how your plants look even in the dead of winter!) Almost every species rose has several of these qualities, enabling me to enjoy the plant long after it has stopped flowering.

When it comes to species roses, I am a foliage freak. All roses retain at least part of their foliage even in the winter, since rose prickles are technically a type of modified leaf. Species rose prickles come in all different sizes, shapes and colors; they can give the stems a soft, furry appearance, or they can lend the plant a fearsome and fiery aspect. As a professional gardener, I'm outside year round, including in winter, when the translucent ruby prickles of *Rosa sericea pteracantha* catch the orange light of the setting sun in the winter and give the plant a fire-like glow at the end of the day.

Other more obvious forms of foliage give the species rose interest throughout the growing season. *Rosa glauca* has a pinkish cast to its otherwise wintergreen foliage. *Rosa rugosa* has rough, almost hairy foliage, and *Rosa spinosissima* has a light, delicate, almost ferny foliage. And this is just in the summer. In autumn the foliage on species roses turns every fall color from yellow to purple.

What's more, the foliage on some plants has a fragrance more luxuriant than the flowers themselves. The new leaves on *Rosa bracteata* and *R. inodora* have a lingering apple scent that fills the garden on a wet or humid day. These are definitely plants that I would choose for my garden.

Like their close relative the apple, roses develop a fruit (called a hip) that starts off green and changes color as it ripens. Hips have an ornamental quality of their own and keep the party going all summer and into the winter after the foliage is gone. Their colors range from a pale limey green to bright pumpkin orange and burgundy. Crack them open when they're ripe for a tasty treat, or pick them off right before the winter and use them in holiday floral arrangements.

The translucent ruby prickles of *Rosa sericea pteracantha* give the plant a fire-like glow at the end of the day.

When it comes right down to it, a species rose is a great plant in either the designed or natural setting. Their flowers are simple and their forms unassuming. They look great, smell good and have a branching pattern that gives the plants presence year round. Even better, they're a snap to care for.

## PLANTING AND MAINTAINING YOUR SPECIES ROSES

Last August, I found myself in a traffic snarl-up on Boston's Southeast Expressway, where the ambient temperature was about 120°F. Looking around, I spotted *Rosa rugosa*, thriving in between two rows of New Jersey barriers in a hideously hostile environment. That one glance wiped out every preconceived notion about the difficulty of rose maintenance. If those roses can not only survive but *flourish* under such extreme conditions, then they can probably do well just about anywhere. Look on the roadside in June and you'll see pink *Rosa virginiana* climbing up into just about anything it can get a purchase on. You'll find

Species roses are relatively disease resistant; several millenia of evolution have produced fit and hardy roses. Above: The new leaves on *Rosa bracteata* have a lingering apple scent that fills the garden on a wet or humid day.

*Rosa palustris* in swampy meadows and *Rosa rugosa* not only in median strips, but growing along the sand dunes on the beach. (In fact, one non-native species rose, *Rosa multiflora,* is such a rampant grower that in many areas it has become an invasive pest, outcompeting the indigenous vegetation.)

The most important thing to keep in mind about growing species roses: They all do best in the sun. There is one thing that you can do right off the bat that will affect the way your rose looks and how it performs for its entire lifetime—site it properly. Your species rose will do fairly well in a wide range of circumstances, but what you want in your garden isn't just any old shrub, but a plant of heretofore unequaled terrestrial splendor. So you've got to find a sunny spot. The soil should be well drained and loamy. A good gauge for this is whether or not grass grows well there. It if does, or could, then you're in luck.

Plant, prune and feed your species rose as you would other roses (for general rose-care tips, see page 32). As for disease, you're in luck: Species roses are relatively disease resistant. This is the major advantage to using unhybridized plants; several millennia of evolution have produced fit and hardy roses. Which isn't to say that all hybrid roses are disease infested—not at all. But species roses do have the genetic cards stacked in their favor in this regard; they may get some of the same diseases that the hybrids get, but it's more likely that they'll survive them without any chemical treatment.

What about Japanese beetles? Again, you're in luck. Japanese beetles don't mature into voracious adult micro-monsters until mid-summer. By this time, most of the species roses have stopped blooming and are producing hips. Japanese beetles are more likely to go where the pickin's are better—like your neighbors' hybrids, which are still in bloom and providing a more succulent meal.

One glance at *Rosa rugosa* not just surviving but flourishing under extreme conditions should wipe out every preconceived notion about the difficulty of maintaining roses.

## FAVORITE SPECIES ROSES

Following is a list of favorite species roses. Some of these are forms of species roses, and some are crosses between two different species, but any lack in purity is more than made up for by garden versatility.

### Small shrubs (2–4 feet tall)

*Rosa spinosissima*—Super flower, foliage and hip producers, with rich green, delicate foliage. Any of its forms or hybrids are worth a try. My favorite is *R. spinosissima altaica*, which at 5 to 6 feet is a bit taller than others of its species, with larger flowers. *Altaica* is packed with white flowers on prominent yellow stems. It's an earlier bloomer, flowering in mid-May and lasting for about three weeks. It then produces beautiful round burgundy hips that are unlike anything else in the late summer and fall garden. All spinosissimas (also known as pimpinellifolias) have a pretty, rich, green and delicate foliage.

*Rosa woodsii*—For those of you with a passion for native North American plants, here's one for you. *Rosa woodsii* is a full shrub, growing to 3 to 4 feet; flowers are blue-pink with a sweet scent. The hips of the woods rose are small and glossy, and the petals are perfect as a garnish on any mid-summer omelette.

*Rosa rugosa*—For anyone who grew up on the coast, this plant is bound to evoke nostalgia and memories of sand in your shoes. This Japanese native has been used so often that, at least in New England, many people think it's a native. It has rough, dark-green leaves and large dark-pink flowers. The scent is sweet, rich and pure. There is a white form called *Rosa rugosa alba,* and the petals of both the pink and white look great as a garnish for your after-dinner finger bowls. My favorite rugosa is *Rosa rugosa* 'Hansa', a large-flowered bloom with a scent that will dominate the area it's planted in.

## Medium shrubs (4–6 feet tall)

*Rosa pendulina*—This plant has it all: beautiful, rich pink flowers; elongated cherry-red hips; and cinnamon-red and yellow stems in the winter. Maximum winter display requires extra pruning in the fall—leave only those canes that look best. This is a labor of love that will satisfy you during those months of dormancy when you normally wouldn't have high expectations for your roses. Underplanting this with *Helleborus foetidus* creates a composition that will never quit.

*Rosa woodsii* has blue-pink flowers with a sweet scent, and small, glossy hips.

25

*Rosa* x *malyi*—I choose this rose on account of its flowers, with their candy-apple petals, white interiors, and bumble-bee yellow stamens. *Rosa* x *malyi* flowers in mid-May, just as spring is driving its hardest back-to-life bargain. This isn't a subtle rose; though it's a one-act show, the smiles it brings are worth everything.

*Rosa* x *hibernica*—This rose is the child of *Rosa spinosissima* and *Rosa canina*. It's also a rose chosen for its flowers, but the flowers wouldn't be nearly as effective without the foliage—a dark and creamy green that backs up dusty pink flowers with a parchment-white interior and yellow stamens.

*Rosa glauca*—Previously named *Rosa rubrifolia* (and for good reason: *rubri* meaning red and *folia* meaning leaf), this American native rose with its wintergreen leaves tinted red is a great foil for any garden featuring dusty or variegated foliage. The flowers are bright pink with white centers, relatively small, and short-lived. The hips, however, start off a pale whitish pink and then turn to orange, a perfect color in the late-summer garden.

The flowers of *Rosa* x *hibernica* wouldn't be nearly as effective without the dark, creamy green foliage.

### Tall shrubs (6–15 feet tall)

&#9758; *Rosa pomifera*—As the botanical name implies, the hips on this rose are like small crab apples. Inconspicuous in flower and almost puritan in winter form, this rose is a big late-summer and early-autumn performer. The hips are almost the size of a quarter and pumpkin yellow in color. Its appearance in the garden is like a broad and bold wash of orange by a painter's brush, totally on the mark.

&#9758; *Rosa beggeriana*—It's not the flowers, hips or scent on this one, but its sheer size. This rose is a monster. Free standing it measures around 13 to 15 feet tall. Few gardens can or will want to support a giant such as this. Size-wise it pushes every limit, while maintaining its presence as a flowering shrub to be admired.

&#9758; *Rosa setigera*—Maybe it's the flowers that come late in the species rose blooming cycle; maybe it's the arching branch form resembling that of a tumbleweed in the winter; maybe it's the pink flowers, borne in clusters, fading to an almost white as they age. Whatever it is, I love this plant. It is vigorous, forthright and unstoppable.

The hips on *Rosa pomifera* are like small crab apples, almost the size of a quarter and pumpkin yellow.

# MINIATURE ROSES

## Portable plants you don't have to bend to tend

### BY SUE FELDBAUM

**Y**EARS AGO when I saw a miniature rose for the first time I thought, "That's nice," and promptly forgot about it. A decade later I happened to take a course on miniature roses and was amazed at the number of sizes, shapes and colors available. That's when I fell for the "little ones."

My tiny garden was already filled to the brim with big roses of every sort: hybrid perpetuals, Bourbons, hybrid teas, floribundas, polyanthas—everything but miniatures. There was no room anywhere in my garden, unquestionably none. But I had to have them, and the only place left was my front porch. "Go for it," I was told. I did.

Now that I had the location for my minis, I had to provide everything they would need to grow well. Sunshine was my biggest challenge—the porch was partially shaded by a large red maple right in front of my house. Pruning the maple hard every two years allowed the minis to get at least four to five hours of sun a day. Providing everything else they needed was easy: pots ( I use 1- to 5- gallon black plastic pots), great soil (my own unscientific formula is one part top-soil, two parts of my very own compost and two parts peat moss), good drainage (shards from clay pots or gravel), heavy mulch (I prefer cedar—it smells good), lots of water (especially on hot days) and a regular spray program against blackspot and mildew (the natural alternative to synthetic chemical fungicides is 1 tablespoon baking soda to 1 gallon water).

I get my minis ready for winter in mid- to late-fall. Beneath my porch is a space we call the "cold room." It is a dark, unheated space made entirely of concrete, with a vent at each end. That's where all the minis are put after I've given them a light pruning. Because it rarely gets below 30° F in the cold room, the plants do well there. All they need is a small drink of water once a month to make sure they don't dry out. I never have any winter kill. About April 15th I bring the minis back outside, and the cycle starts anew.

Just like big roses, minis have a variety of growth habits. 'Lavender Jewel' has dark foliage and compact, bushy growth.

The advantages of growing miniature roses in pots are many and varied. Here are my own top three reasons:

**No bending.** My miniature rose collection has grown to 40 cultivars planted in 60 individual pots. The pots are arranged on plastic crates across the south end of the porch, creating a three-tiered bank. This setup makes housekeeping and pruning simple. I merely place a pot on an old wooden lazy Susan that I keep on the porch table, pull up a comfortable chair and work on my roses while seated.

**Mobility.** Although the roses are not necessarily at their peak at the same time, my porch garden always looks great because I can move individual roses around for an outstanding show any time during the season. I can also create different color combinations whenever I like. And, best of all, instead of cutting blooms for the house, I can bring a whole plant inside for a while without damaging it in the slightest.

⚜ **Friends, Neighbors and Strangers.** Anyone who showers a garden with love and attention will understand how thrilled I am when passersby ooh and ahh over my miniature rose collection. Neighbors have asked for advice before rushing out to buy their own minis. One friend who has a few miniatures in pots asked if I would take care of them while she is away for a while. I said, "Sure, bring them over!" (And she'll do the same for me.)

Here's one important thing to keep in mind about minis: Just like big roses they have a variety of growth habits. That tiny plant that arrives at your doorstep from a mail order nursery could grow into a formidable mini shrub (like 'Gourmet Popcorn'), or a high- and wide-ranging climber (like 'Jeanne Lajoie') or remain delicate and small (like 'Cinderella'). How to tell in advance? Often the nursery catalog will include a description of the mature plant. You can also check rose books, and visit local public gardens. It's helpful to know the size of a full-grown plant when you're planning your moveable garden so you can choose the right pot. ⚜

## 10 FAVORITE MINIATURE ROSES

**'Cinderella'**—White micromini. Compact and bushy all the time.

**'Dresden Doll'**—Moss, light pink. Most beautiful when just opened.

**'Green Ice'**—White to green. Always in flower, good in a hanging basket.

**'Little Artist'**—Red with white center. Semi-double and delightful.

**'Mountie'**—Medium red. Non-stop blooms.

**'Rise 'n Shine'**—Medium yellow. Tall, clustered and very upright.

**'Rouletii'**—Medium pink. This started it all. I just like it.

**'Sachet'**—Mauve. Most fragrant, long-lasting blooms.

**'Si'**—Micromini. White. There isn't a smaller rose.

**'Teddy Bear'**—Russet. An interesting color.

**'RISE 'N SHINE'**

**'POPCORN'**

**'CINDERELLA'**

**R. ROULETII**

**'LITTLE ARTIST'**

**'GREEN ICE'**

# CHEMICAL-FREE ROSE CARE

### BY LIZ DRUITT

**I**N THE WILD, no one sprays the roses. The Louisiana swamps produce healthy roses without human supervision. Along the rugged seacoasts of Japan and in the sturdy hedgerows of the British isles, roses bloom and fruit without a weekly pesticidal sacrament. So why, in our gardens, do roses rank right up there with lawn grasses as having the greatest chemical dependency and the highest maintenance requirement of anything in the yard? Are garden rose varieties honestly so much more fragile than their wild sisters?

Some really are, in part because for years competitive gardeners selected plants for flower characteristics over general vigor. Growers had to turn out masses of these plants, whose genetic viability was questionable, in order to survive financially. But as the 20th century ends and the pesticides to support weak roses fall from favor (and availability), this is changing.

Individual rose breeders, already used to thinking ten years ahead of the rest of us, are working to bring out new roses that are both garden worthy (that is, healthy) and exhibition worthy (that is, gorgeous). The American Rose Society is adapting its focus to support new rose varieties that are more pest and disease resistant and to encourage environmentally sound cultivation techniques. Groups like the Heritage Rose Foundation are working to make sure that vigorous old-rose varieties surviving in cemeteries, public and private garden collections and forgotten crannies are preserved for use as breeding stock and re-introduced into commerce. But it's up to individual gardeners to make these efforts worthwhile, by changing the way we grow roses on our own properties. Here are some ways to enhance your roses' ability to take care of themselves:

🌀 **Begin with proper site selection.** With a few exceptions (see "Landscaping With Roses," page 42), roses need plenty of direct sun. Anything less and roses are likely to languish; they certainly won't bloom to their full potential. Good air circulation around your roses is essential to keep down blackspot and

Don't segregate your roses. This is like ringing a dinner bell for the pests that love them. Mixing roses with other plants can help slow down a potential pest population explosion.

other fungal diseases. Healthy soil is critical as well. A standard mixture is one part existing topsoil, one part sand and one part organic material, ideally in raised beds at least 6 inches high for enhanced drainage. Even if you can't hand-mix your soil, try to create raised beds with existing soil and nurture soil organisms with regular applications of composts, mulches, natural fertilizers and water. Healthy soil means healthy roots and good nutrition for your roses.

**Select the right plants.** When selecting roses, make sure any variety that catches your eye is not particularly prone to blackspot, powdery mildew, rust or any other disease that is prevalent in your area. In fact, make a point of seeking out disease-resistant varieties. Look, too, for regionally adapted roses, those suited to your climate and conditions. This handbook lists some of the best performers for various regions. Ask around your neighborhood for suggestions, too; gardeners who grow roses locally will have better ideas about what works in your area than nurseries that import stock from large, out-of-state growers.

**Diversify your plantings.** Don't make a garden exclusively with roses. This is like ringing a dinner bell for the pests that love them. Instead, design your garden with a diverse array of healthy plants. Many pests and disease pathogens spread like wildfire from one plant to another, and so mixing up the planting can slow down the pest population explosion. Also try using roses from different classes, as they have varied natural susceptibility to specific types of problems.

**Make your garden a haven for beneficial insects.** These are not only functional—they prey on or parasitize pests—they're also fun, and educational to boot. Most suppliers (both mail-order companies and, increasingly, local garden centers) can give you information on suitable varieties and how to get them estab-

Raised beds (at least 6 inches high) provide enhanced drainage.

lished. For starters, try lacewings; the adults and especially the larvae (the immature caterpillar-like stage) consume aphids, scales, mites and other pests voraciously. Or lady beetles (better known as ladybugs); most suppliers offer the adult beetles, but the larvae eat more aphids than even the adults do. To encourage them to stick around long enough to lay eggs that will hatch into hungry larvae, plant their favorite herbs and flowers (see below).

As you learn the quirks of various types of beneficial insects and release more in your garden, you'll be re-establishing healthy, balanced populations within your whole neighborhood. Try to discourage your neighbors from using pesticides that will kill your new pets. Chip in together for beneficial insects and make their release a community event. Get kids who have to do biology projects to figure out what the most common local garden pests are and what predators will best control them.

🌹 **Grow nectar and shelter plants.** How are your beneficial insects going to live between waves of pests? They need certain kinds of plants for shelter and food. If you don't have a wildflower area close by and don't, for some reason, want to plant one around your garden, there are still several options. Consider working with your neighborhood association to turn any vacant lots into wildflower meadows, encouraging a healthy balance of insect life in the immediate area. Everybody's garden will benefit. Within your own garden, include tansy, dill, fennel, catnip, yarrow, butterfly weed (*Asclepias tuberosa*), coreopsis, gaillardias, asters, marigolds and a few goldenrod plants—all of which are attractive to one or more beneficial insects. The more invasive of these (tansy, yarrow, goldenrod) can be kept under control by planting them in pots.

🌹 **Experiment with "companion" plantings.** Although there is often no hard scientific evidence to back up their observations, some gardeners have found that certain plants have a deterrent effect on specific pests and diseases. I personally have had success in my rose garden with alliums (the garlic and onion family), catnip, thyme, rosemary, wormwood (not *Artemisia absinthium*, which is strongly allelopathic—that is, it secretes substances harmful to other plants), southernwood, alyssum, tansy, coriander, fennel, nasturtiums, petunias, mint and geraniums. You may want to experiment, grouping combinations of these, especially the first six, around susceptible roses. Again, you can grow the more invasive varieties in containers to keep them from spreading.

🌹 **Use hedgerows and barriers to repel pests.** A windbreak of some kind will keep a number of bugs out of your garden. Lightly motivated or low-flying species can

Lady beetle larvae eat even more aphids than the adults do.

be deterred by a physical barrier close to the plants of their choice. Consider your property as a whole: Why plant in the center of the yard, when you can make your privacy fence work as a natural pest control? Does the wall of your house block the prevailing wind—and with it prevailing pests? A shed, even a row of sunflowers, can serve the same function.

🌹 **Use alternative sprays, but only as a last resort.** If you must spray, be gentle. Foliar feeding with compost tea or fish emulsion and seaweed will give your roses a vitality boost that may help them throw off a pest or disease problem on their own. A simple hard water spray that washes above and below the leaves can knock off a lot of pests and even fungus spores (as well as the beneficial insects, so keep an eye out for them). Use a baking soda solution for fungal diseases like blackspot (see "Nine Top Rose Pests," page 36). Insecticidal soaps are very effective for knocking back high levels of pests while waiting for the beneficial insects to arrive. Keep in mind, though, that they must be sprayed directly on the pests to be effective.

🌹 **Don't demand total perfection in your roses.** Learn to see beauty in good health overall; total perfection is unnatural. It's possible to grow show-quality blooms on a bush that has blackspot on a few leaves. Discovering the difference between a balanced situation and a serious blight will save a lot of stress and effort and give you more time to genuinely appreciate your garden and the world around it.　　　　　　　　　　　　　　　　　　🌹

# Nine Top Rose Pests and Pathogens

## A quick guide to chemical-free control

The adage "an ounce of prevention is worth a pound of cure" holds especially true in chemical-free rose care. The best offense against rose pests and pathogens is defense: Buy healthy, disease-resistant roses and be diligent about hygiene and preventive maintenance, such as destroying diseased foliage and flowers and cleaning up around your rose bushes in the fall.

**1** **Aphids**—Tiny (1/16" to 5/16" in length), pear-shaped, typically yellow-green insects that suck sap from the stems, leaves or roots of host plants. Clusters of feeding aphids cause stunting and deformation of leaves and stems and produce copious amounts of honeydew, a sticky, sugary liquid. Aphids are eaten by lady beetles, lacewings and many other predators. You can knock them off your plants with jets of water. Insecticidal soaps are also effective.

**2** **Blackspot**—Probably the most widely distributed and serious rose disease, blackspot is a fungal disease named for the black spots that develop on upper leaf surfaces. Leaf tissue surrounding the spots turns yellow, expanding until the leaf drops. Good air circulation keeps blackspot spores from germinating. Avoid excessive watering during cloudy and humid weather. Look for resistant rose varieties. Practicing good hygiene is critical: Remove affected leaves and branches to reduce overwintering of the pathogen. You can also spray susceptible plants every five days with a baking soda solution (one tablespoon of baking soda and a few drops of horticultural oil or Ivory soap to one gallon of water).

**3** **Borers**—Larvae of rose-stem girdler, rose-stem sawfly and carpenter bees bore holes in canes, causing new growth to wilt. Control borers by cutting off the infected canes below the end of the hole.

**4** **Downy mildew**—A fungal disease with many of the same symptoms as blackspot, but usually starting at the top of the bush rather than the bottom. Downy mildew attacks young leaves and stems of flowers. Infected leaves develop

Troubles, from left to right: Blackspot, powdery mildew and rose midge damage

irregular, purple-red spots. Leaflets may turn yellow, and leaf drop can be severe. Preventive measures are the same as with blackspot. To avoid excessive moisture on the leaves (especially in cool weather), allow plenty of space among plants for good air circulation. Some gardeners are also experimenting with warm water sprays. And in cold climates, you can help control downy mildew by spraying with horticultural oil early in the spring when you prune your roses.

**5** **Japanese beetles**—Oval-shaped, 1/2"-long, metallic green beetles with copper-colored wings. The larva, or grub, is grayish white and 1/2" to 1" long. The adult beetles rapidly skeletonize foliage and disfigure flowers. Hand picking is the most effective way to keep beetles off your roses. (Traps often do more harm than good by attracting large numbers of beetles to your yard.) You can keep future beetle populations in check by controlling large infestations of larvae (grubs) in your lawn with parasitic nematodes and milky spore (*Bacillus popilliae*), a bacterium that causes a lethal disease specific to Japanese beetle grubs.

**6** **Powdery mildew**—A fungus that appears as powdery white growth on the surfaces of young leaves, which become twisted and distorted. Older leaves may not be distorted, but areas may be covered with the growth of the mildew fungus. Planting resistant rose cultivars can help. Spraying with a baking soda solution (see blackspot, above) prevents and controls powdery mildew. Prune and destroy all infected parts. In regions where winters are severe, rake and destroy fallen leaves from around the bushes at the end of the season and destroy them .

**7** **Rose midges**—Very tiny white maggots that hatch from eggs laid by adult insects on new growth and under the sepals of flower buds. The maggots feed on new growth, causing deformed, blackened buds and leaves. Crisp, burned-looking foliage tips are the first sign of midge infestation; you can help control midges by examining your roses daily in the early spring and early fall, and pruning and destroying all damaged parts.

**8**    **Spider mites**—So small (1/64" to 1/32" long) that they're difficult to detect without a hand lens, spider mites puncture plant tissue and feed on the sap, causing severe yellowing of leaves and premature leaf death. Prune heavily infested branches to slow the spread of these pests. Spider mites and their webbing can be washed off with jets of water. They are parasitised by commercially available predatory

## PRUNING EASY-CARE ROSES

P roper pruning is an important part of chemical-free rose care. All roses, with the exception of species roses and the non-repeating old garden roses, should be pruned at the beginning of the growing season. Rose bushes that are left unpruned will be less productive and more prone to insects and diseases.

The best time to prune your roses is in the early spring. This is when the buds are just about to burst open and the stems are all still clearly visible. Also, the weather in spring is still cool enough to allow you to be comfortable in a long-sleeve shirt. Woe to the rose pruner who works in short sleeves!

Always use the sharpest and cleanest pruning shears that you can. Here are the main considerations:

🌹 Look for weak, small growth that will not support bloom. Such growth is often where disease begins, and so it should be removed. Healthy growth is rarely infested initially, unless it is near the weaker stems.

🌹 As roses mature they become crowded with dead wood; cutting out such branches constitutes the majority of pruning that you will do. Dead wood

Make cut at a 45° angle, about 1/4 inch above a swelling or newly breaking bud. When deadheading (opposite page), cut spent bloom to just above the node of a leaf composed of five leaflets.

mites. Horticultural oils and insecticidal soaps provide some control.

**9** **Thrips**—Extremely tiny (1/50" to 1/25" long) insects that creep into the flower buds and begin feeding on them. The buds may brown out and refuse to open; if they do open, the flowers may have brown edges. Thrips are eaten by lacewings, minute pirate bugs, predatory mites and insect-eating nematodes. Populations can be monitored and in some cases controlled with sticky traps. These pests don't like wet conditions and can be drowned easily, so water sprays will keep populations down. Insecticidal soap may help with serious infestations. ✿

can be distinguished by an absence of buds.

✿ Roses need air circulation. Open up the center of the plant by removing cluttered canes. Cut out any canes that cross each other.

✿ As canes get older, they will get leggy and produce fewer and fewer flowers. You will recognize these canes by their discolored and cracked bark at the base. Prune them to the ground.

✿ The lower you prune modern shrub-type roses such as floribundas, grandifloras, polyanthas and hybrid teas, the stronger the new growth will be. Modern shrub types that are heavily pruned will develop good basal breaks, the strong canes from the base of the plant that produce the best flowers.

✿ Make cuts at a 45° angle, about 1/4 inch above swelling or newly breaking buds.

✿ At any time of year you may notice that a branch suddenly dies back and all of the leaves remaining on the stem turn brown and withered, or yellow and splotchy. In other cases, you might see abnormalities in the stem called galls, formed when an insect lays its eggs within the bark. To keep the problem from spreading, cut these sections out with clean pruners, wiping the blade with disinfectant after each cut.

✿ Deadheading faded flowers is another important part of pruning. Cut spent blooms to just above the node of a leaf composed of five leaflets.

# DRIP IRRIGATION FOR ROSES

### BY OZ AND AUDREY OSBORN

**W**hen we first started growing roses, we had a very simple method: read a rose catalog, order several roses, wait for them to arrive, plant them, read another catalog and order some more roses.

But those beautiful pictures in the catalog and the equally magnificent blooms in our garden were getting us in over our heads. Sure, we could take care of the 20 roses we had the first year, but the 20 grew to 50, 50 became 100 and then 300.

Our love of roses had become a "labor" of love that left us very little time to stop and actually smell the roses. Most of our time was consumed watering the plants. While it's very relaxing to lazily water a rosebush with an old-fashioned 2-gallon watering can, this method was simply no longer practical for us.

After asking around, we found an alternative that not only saves us time, but also helps prevent blackspot and mildew in our humid New Jersey climate. The irrigation system consists of two elements: simple rolls of 3/4-inch poly-pipe available at major home-supply stores, and drip rings with a 24-inch water tube, available from garden-supply companies.

Each rose has its own drip ring, which you attach to the poly-pipe with a tool that's very similar to an ice-pick. You can cut the poly-pipe to any desired length with a bread knife or even with your rose clippers. Plastic connectors (either T-, L- or Y-shaped) are easily hammered into the poly-pipe to allow any design you wish.

With only one outdoor water spigot, this system gives equal amounts of water to both the roses closest to our house and those farthest away. The entire system is connected to the water line through a battery-operated timer, which is activated twice a day for 30 minutes. A good timer will also have an override feature that enables you to extend the watering time during extremely dry weather. ❀

Left: Drip irrigation can save time and keep down diseases.
Opposite page: Applying deer psychology results in a foolproof, aesthetically pleasing deer fence.

# KEEPING DEER AT BAY

BY JOYCE DEMITS

**M**y sister, Virginia, and I started a small historical heritage-rose collection at the Mendocino Coast Botanical Gardens in Fort Bragg, California. For deer control we first used electrical fencing—which didn't look good *or* protect the roses from deer. By applying some deer psychology, we came up with a fairly foolproof and aesthetically pleasing deer fence.

The solution involved constructing sections of fence 8 feet wide by 4 feet high, assembled in a staggered pattern—the second section 18 inches in from the first section, the third section back in line with the first, and so on. Breaking up the straight line of fencing confuses the deer, because they have a hard time gauging where to jump. Each section was built individually, using 2-by-4s for the horizontal rails. The pickets were 1-by-4s, spaced 2 inches apart. They could also be set farther apart and still deter the deer. The supporting posts were 6-foot long 4-by-4s, set into the ground 18 inches deep, and the completed fence sections were attached to these. The posts stand 6 inches above the height of the pickets.

Horizontal spreaders between the 8-foot sections were constructed of 1-by-2s, with 6 inches of space between them from the ground up to the top horizontal rail. Round porcelain insulators were nailed onto the top of the posts and electric wire was strung for a temporary deterrent all the way around, 6 inches above the pickets.

Deer are afraid to jump into a space where they can't see where they're going to land, so we planted large, dense shrub roses around the inside periphery of the fence. Some good choices of spreading roses are the hybrid Chinas ("Nathalie's High Hills," 'Paul Ricault' and "Homestead"); hybrid albas ('Madame Plantier' and 'Belle Amour'); 'Königin von Dänemark', 'Félicité Parmentier' and 'Fortune's Double Yellow'; and repeating roses 'William Jesse', 'Magna Charta', and *Rosa damascena bifera*. Warmer climates would be conducive to growing Chinas.

Once the roses covered the space inside the fence, we didn't need the hot wire as a deterrent, and we disconnected it. Deer haven't gotten into the garden except when the gate was left open.  🌹

**41**

# LANDSCAPING WITH ROSES

### BY GREGG LOWERY

**W**HETHER YOUR IDEAL GARDEN is geometric and crisp, informal and flowery or wild and serene, there is a place in it for roses. Screens and hedges, flowering mounds and carpets, shady bowers of fragrance, crisp path edgings, elegant columns of flowers, foliage fine and ferny or rich green and lustrous—these and a hundred more effects can be created with roses.

## ROSES FOR FORM, TEXTURE AND FOLIAGE

No matter how you use them in your garden, you would be wise to keep in mind that much of the year roses are leafy shrubs. Their shapes make a green presence in the garden. You can use these forms, as well as the textures and tints of the foliage, to harmonize with other ornamental plants. Some roses are best used as large shrubs or tall hedges. Others grow naturally into compact shrubs. Still others make excellent groundcovers. Climbers and ramblers play a dramatic role in providing a backdrop for other plants and in shaping the garden's vertical dimension.

### LARGE SHRUBS

The largest of the roses become impressive shrubs 5 to 12 feet high and almost as wide.

All too seldom seen in modern gardens, the wild or species roses are handsome as single specimens and in massed plantings. The ancestral parent of our North American species, *Rosa cinnamomea*, is a tall, very graceful shrub whose cinnamon-brown stems liven up the winter garden. The prairie rose, *Rosa setigera*, has broad, soft leaves, and is often mistaken for bramble or berry foliage. The latest-blooming American wild rose, it makes a handsome companion to late summer perennials.

The centifolias, which grow in arching fountains to about 6 feet, epitomize the traditional cottage garden.

*Rosa moschata*, the musk rose, is suited to the humid summers of the southern states. It, too, makes a handsome large shrub, upright to about 6 feet and spreading. Its pure white flowers in great clusters open successively over many months, beginning in mid-summer, and their scent, rich, exotic and sweet, laces the air on a warm, moist day. But perhaps its greatest asset is its abundant downy, gray-green foliage, so effective in a dense planting of dark greens, such as those of yew and bay.

The albas are tall, arching shrubs with sweetly scented flowers in white or pale pink. Their pale, gray-green foliage is a standout in any garden setting. Damask roses are broadly arching plants whose flowers crowd closely in large clusters and are so strongly perfumed they scent the surrounding air. Two notable examples are the repeat-blooming 'Autumn Damask' and its mossy, white-flowered offspring, 'Quatre Saisons Blanc Mousseux'.

The centifolias grow in modest arching fountains to about 6 feet, are luxuriant in leaf and feature globular flowers with fine-textured petals and a heady fragrance. They epitomize the traditional cottage garden, looking their best when herbs and perennial flowers crowd around them. The moss roses tend to be large plants, stout of stem and very thorny. Some are tall and upright, while others form dense, crowded thickets. The pungent "moss" that covers their flower buds, like the fragrant leaves of scented geraniums, is best appreciated at the tips of your fingers. Plant them near a path, where even a tall-growing moss like 'Mrs. William Paul' can best be enjoyed at close range.

The hybrid Chinas are vigorous shrubs. They have fragrant, full-petaled flowers, reminiscent of the old roses, but unlike their European ancestors they offer smooth foliage, rather smooth stems and a tendency to produce some later flowers. 'Mme. Plantier', among the most famous, makes a graceful fountain of very fragrant double white flowers, ideal for planting beneath a fruit tree where it will reach up and wreathe the branches with its beauty.

The tea roses are not for every American climate, but their legion of hybrids remains today the most successful group of roses to grow in the humid southern states, and they also excel in California. These roses run the gamut from large to compact. The brilliant pink 'Bon Silène' smothers itself with flowers up to 12 months of the year, building into a big, elegant shrub.

The hybrid perpetuals and the Bourbons can be roughly divided into the large though compact growers and the open, arching growers. Typical of the compact-growing Bourbons is 'Honorine de Brabant', which is slender of stem, smooth of wood and foliage, growing to 5 or 6 feet with each new growth ending in a flower cluster. The stouter of the hybrid perpetuals have heavier canes, with more thorns and less waxy foliage. 'La Reine', at the smaller end of the scale, grows to 5 feet, producing globular, deep pink blooms all summer. 'Frau Karl Druschki', long admired for its pure white flowers, is an exaggeration of vigor, building mightily like a lilac to 7 to 10 feet. These shrubby Bourbons and hybrid perpetuals are easy to use in the garden, as specimens, hedges or mid- to back-border shrubs in a mixed planting.

The open, arching growers among the Bourbons and hybrid perpetuals, like the silvery pink hybrid perpetual, 'Arrillaga', or the raspberry-scented Bourbon, 'Mme. Isaac Pereire', produce long canes that rise up and arch out. Their natural fountain shape can be lovely in the garden.

## COMPACT SHRUBS

By "compact" I refer to roses that can be kept to less than 5 feet tall and 4 feet wide. These roses tend to have dense foliage throughout the bush, not just on the outside, and they bloom nearly to the ground, as well as at the top. Gardeners seeking a more tailored effect will find these shrubs useful and handsome.

Many of the wild roses are modest growers. *Rosa spinosissima* has tiny, fern-like foliage and dramatic, shiny black hips.

They serve well in place of broad-leafed evergreens, in foundation plantings, as crisp hedges or in formal pairs or groups.

Many of the wild roses are modest growers that fit elegantly in even the most urban settings. A great favorite of mine is the Scots brier, *Rosa spinosissima,* whose very tiny, fern-like foliage and shiny black fruits are dramatic. One fine hybrid, 'Doorenbos Selection', stays very low, to about 2-1/2 feet, suckering densely to 3 feet or more. For weeks in early summer it blooms with single, grape-purple saucers lit with golden stamens, the delight of bees and hummingbirds.

Among the most compact of the Bourbons, at just 2-1/2 feet tall, is 'Souvenir de la Malmaison', a rose by now so familiar to American gardeners that many assume all Bourbons form low shrubs with good, long, cutting stems. Some tea roses also make excellent compact shrubs. For example, 'Mme. Lambard', whose subtle colorings of coffee, cream and pink blend and change with the weather, grows about 4-1/2 feet high. As floriferous as the teas, and also most suitable for mild climates, are the Chinas, compact plants whose pinks and cherry reds bloom in a continuous stream. Chinas like 'Old Blush' and 'Cramoisi Supérieur' are so floriferous, in fact, that they have come to be known as the monthly roses.

## GROUNDCOVERS

When most gardeners think of groundcovers, they think of lawn, or perhaps a low-growing herb like thyme. Here I'm using the term in the broader sense—that is, a plant that is not necessarily close-cropped but does form a dense, fairly weed-proof cover. Roses in this category range in growth habit from relatively ground-hugging to low-mounding forms. *Rosa wichuraiana porteriifolia*, a hardy, very late-blooming variety from Japan with single, white flowers, rarely grows above 12 inches tall but spreads as much as 20 feet. Among the most notable low-mounding rose are the gallicas. These mostly short-growing, thicket-forming plants can be grouped in masses to cover sloping or level ground.

Some of the best groundcovers are those developed from the wild Japanese rose, *Rosa rugosa*. The rugosa's foliage resists all rose diseases. And because rugosas are very dense growers, forming thickets when on their own roots, they are excellent for mass plantings. On sloping ground and in sandy soils they control erosion. Two low-growing rugosas are 'Frau Dagmar Hartopp', a single pink older variety and 'Jens Munk', a newer hybrid in rich cerise pink.

Recent efforts of Meilland in France, Lens of Belgium and the Poulsens in Denmark have focused on creating a new race of ground-covering roses that are healthy, carefree and repeat-blooming.

## HEDGES

Many of the larger roses, such as the species *Rosa cinnamomea* and *R. moschata*, make elegant, informal hedges when left unsheared. Damask roses, well armed with prickles, are also good candidates for a tall hedge. One good choice is 'Gloire de Guilan', which spreads from 5 to 6 feet wide in a dense, mounding shape and features highly perfumed, medium pink flowers. You might also consider the more compact of the hybrid perpetuals and Bourbons, as well as the hybrid musks. The Noisettes make medium-height hedges, 5 or so feet tall; these are best pruned to some degree for shape. Polyanthas and miniature roses, sheared or unsheared, can serve as lower-growing hedges. In formal gardens, the rugosas can be tightly sheared as medium to tall hedges.

## CLIMBERS AND RAMBLERS

Trees and tall shrubs are essential ingredients in the garden because they provide a background of green and shape the air above. Climbers and ramblers can serve the same purpose. Walls and fences are ideal hosts for these long-caned roses, which can be trained tightly with the use of wires or trelliswork, or allowed to cascade freely from fencetops and roofs. In formal and informal settings roses make delightful freestanding pillars, their canes spiraling up wood or brick posts, wrought-iron or galvanized pipes or stone columns. Simple small arches or arbors are ideal for training climbing roses, and create elegant focal points in the garden, especially to mark entrances or terminate pathways. In larger gardens a long series of arbors provides drama to a walkway and a means of linking separate spaces in the garden. Vigorous ramblers like 'Newport Fairy' or species like *Rosa brunonii* 'La Mortola' will scramble up trees, festooning them with color in early summer.

Climbing roses such as 'Dortmund' can be elegant focal points.

Too little has been done in the development of climbing roses in the past 50 years. Climbing sports of hybrid teas like 'Peace' are readily available from retail nurseries, but these are generally very heavy of cane and poor repeat-bloomers, neither flexible enough to train nor worthy of the space they take. A handful of older climbing hybrid teas are excellent, including 'Crimson Glory', 'Kaiserin Auguste Viktoria', 'Golden Dawn', 'La France', 'Mme. Caroline Testout', 'Mme. Jules Bouché', 'Mrs. Sam McGredy', 'Radiance', 'Snowbird' and 'Talisman'.

For the greatest selection of good climbers, look among the old classes. Hybrids of *Rosa wichuraiana* are true ramblers with long, lithe, flexible canes, glossy foliage of good health, and medium to large flowers in a wide range of colors and floral forms. The worthy attributes of hybrids like 'Dr. Van Fleet' and 'Mary Wallace' were used later in breeding excellent hardy climbers such as 'Coral Creeper' and 'Mrs. Arthur Curtis James'. These are less flexible than their ancestors and more manageable, while equally healthy and handsome of foliage.

Don't forget the larger, arching growers found among the Bourbon and hybrid

'Mary Rose'. This and other David Austin roses hark back to a 19th-century standard of perfection.

perpetual roses when you look for climbers. These are generally not very large growers, but varieties like the Bourbon 'Mme. Ernest Calvat' and the hybrid perpetual 'Général Jacqueminot' can do justice to a small arch or arbor. They can not only be trained onto arches and pillars, walls and fences, but also "pegged" to the ground as was the fashion in late Victorian gardens, to make a broad mound or carpet of bloom.

Gardeners in mild climates can grow the most extraordinary group of climbing roses, the Noisettes. The early Noisette hybrids grow much like their wild-rose parent, *Rosa moschata*, forming upright, spreading shrubs. However, they can be trained with little difficulty to ascend a pillar or arch. Such sweetly fragrant roses as 'Champneys' Pink Cluster' and 'Blush Noisette' bloom so steadily and in such profusion that they would be grown by all American gardeners were they more cold hardy. The tea-Noisettes, like 'Mme. Alfred Carrière', are larger climbers that produce moderate to long canes and can be trained to larger structures and onto rooftops and very high walls. They, too, are the glories of warm gardens of the South and the West.

## ROSES FOR FLOWERS

We have seen how the growth habit and foliage of many roses can enhance the garden. Gardeners most often select varieties for their flowers. It is useful to distinguish between roses that are chosen for the beauty of their flowers, and those grown for their overall flowering effect in the garden.

### LARGE-FLOWERED ROSES

Hybrid teas, the largest class of roses, have been developed for the perfection of individual flowers. So, too, have the new English roses, hybridized by David

Austin. The standard of beauty epitomized in the hybrid tea rose is the high-centered or pointed bud which, half-open, creates an elegant spiral of petals. Typical of this floral style are hybrid teas such as 'Pristine', 'Ophelia' and 'Eclipse'. In old-fashioned flower forms, it's the fully opened bloom that is most admired. David Austin's English roses hark back to this 19th-century standard of perfection. The flat flowers of the soft pink 'Claire' rose contain 100 petals or more.

## CLUSTER-FLOWERED ROSES

Clustering has long been the rule rather than the exception with roses, but the trait has been encouraged and developed in modern roses more than ever before. This began with the polyanthas in the late 1800's; one of the most exquisite is 'Marie Pavié', whose double, white, scented blooms appear in what seems an endless succession. Its low stature and luxurious foliage make it an ideal subject for the front of the border or a well positioned terra-cotta pot. Polyanthas, among the most versatile of garden plants, can be used as low hedges, companions to herbaceous perennials or massed in a bed. Their range of subtle colors is delightful, from the soft salmon blush of 'Marytje Cazant', to the coral pink of 'Margo Koster' and the deep grape purple of 'Baby Faurax'.

Although their parentage is similar to that of the polyanthas, the hybrid musk roses are larger, becoming shrubs of 4 to 6 feet tall and as wide. Many, like the single white 'Kathleen' and the double blush 'Bubble Bath', are extremely fragrant. Hybrid musks are used widely in Britain and Europe, either grown in their natural arching forms, trained as small climbers or grouped along fence lines as everblooming hedges. They bloom in clusters with flowers small and rosette-like, as in the purple 'Excellenz von Schubert', or large and very double like the scented apricot flowers of 'Buff Beauty'.

## ROSES FOR SHADE

Another remarkable feature of the hybrid musks is their general tolerance of shade. Generally those with smaller, less double flowers grow and bloom well with little direct sun. The best, without a doubt, are 'Kathleen', 'Bubble Bath' and the single, pale pink 'Ballerina', whose large domed heads of flowers are reminiscent of hydrangeas. While hybrid musks are suitable for a range of climates, shade gardeners in warm regions can also choose among the Noisettes. Like the hybrid musks, the Noisettes do not require direct sun to be healthy and bloom, but both do need bright, indirect light, such as that found on the north side of a house or under a high tree canopy.

# A MIXED GARDEN WITH ROSES

BY JOHN AND MARIE BUTLER

**M**any gardeners think of the rose garden as an entity in and of itself, separate from the herb garden, kitchen garden or flower border. For us, though, the object of making a garden is to have plants in bloom as much as possible throughout most of the year. Grow the old garden roses that blossom abundantly and luxuriantly in the spring and then fall quiet, and combine them with shrubs, perennials, annuals, bulbs, native wildflowers and even vegetables to ensure pleasing bloom and interesting foliage in all seasons. The various plants must complement the roses, allow for colors appropriate to the particular season and afford contrasts of form and leaf. There's nothing quite as exuberant as a garden in which roses mingle freely with a profusion of other plants.

The overall design of our own garden, on about two acres in central Virginia, is formal, with alleés, borders and parterres. There is a central allée, mostly a grass walkway, that runs 200 feet between formal hedges of clipped elaeagnus 8 feet tall. Between these hedges are five major garden "rooms" connected by grass or gravel walks edged with bricks. Within this geometric framework is essentially a garden of old roses underplanted with perennials, herbs and bulbs in the colonial cottage garden style of the Tidewater region.

We have learned that while the old garden roses are beautiful in themselves, they are much more pleasing when grown with other plants of muted colors and varying forms. With the graceful, mounding forms of damasks, gallicas and centifolias, plants with spike-shaped blooms are most pleasing. In May, various foxgloves are indispensable for providing vertical interest. Salsify (*Tragopogon porrifolius*) opens its purple blooms in the morning but closes by noon. Camassias offer wands of blue and lavender, followed by a tapestry of deep blue, purple and white irises. At midsummer, spikes of bellflower, anise hyssop, *Nicotiana sylvestris*, balloon flower, hollyhock and salvias parade through the borders among the pastel roses. Still later come blazing-star, plume poppy, ironweed and tartarian aster. Billows of silver-leaved artemisias, lamb's-ears and lavenders petticoat the often bare ankles of some of the old roses.

Within the geometric framework of John and Marie Butler's garden are old roses underplanted with perennials, herbs and bulbs in the colonial cottage garden style.

Among the hybrid musk roses with their warm buff yellow, creamy whites and warm pinks we also grow plants with white, blue, lavender and purple blooms, including Stokes' aster, *Clematis heracleifolia* and various catmints. When the roses rest at midsummer, we enjoy the flowers of daylilies.

Among the tea roses, some of which grow to 7 feet tall and quite wide, we treasure old varieties of pinks. Columbines, thymes, verbenas, penstemons, pelargoniums and other flowers also bloom among these most delicate, refined and exquisite roses, the preeminent roses for the South.

Native wildflowers that meet our requirements for muted colors and graceful forms also mingle with the roses throughout the garden. Scullcaps (*Scutellaria integrifolia* and the later-blooming *S. incana*), meadow beauty (*Rhexia mariana purpurea*) and a native clematis (*Clematis viorna*) are some of our favorites. *Euphorbia corollata*, our "baby's breath," blooms pristinely in late summer among all the roses. Airy white bedstraw, another "baby's breath," cloaks the ankles of the Noisettes and climbing teas. And the season closes with vibrant displays of asters in shades of purple, lavender and white among the autumn blooms of the Noisettes, hybrid musks, tea roses and old hybrid teas.

# EASY-CARE ROSES BY REGION

In the pages that follow, rosarians from diverse climates, from sultry southern Texas to the frigid mountaintops of Vermont, offer their personal insights into growing roses. At the end of each regional section, you'll find 15 recommended roses that are both gorgeous and easy to grow.

# Reminiscences to Riches

BY RICHARD A. KLINGENSMITH

Roses have been part of my life for almost 60 years. My first memory of roses was an olfactory imprint made by the 'Seven Sisters' growing in my grandmother's garden in Fruitland, Idaho. Some 55 years later, 'Seven Sisters' still arouses sentimental memories of my late mother, Rose, and her own six sisters, who were nurtured on the very soil where my grandmother taught me the basics I apply today, with minor exceptions, in my own backyard in Belle Harbor, New York. Although my grandmother's garden was set amid acres of well-sprayed orchards, my garden thrives (without insecticides) on a sand bar where, for centuries, only sandfleas flourished.

Gradually, over a 20-year period, I have transformed 625 square feet on Rockaway Peninsula, a barrier island of sand and salt air, into a heavy-yielding, high-intensity garden. At first my plot, more like a sandbox covered by a mere inch of "soil," grew only weak, sickly plants destined to be devoured by insects of all kinds. Over the years, it has evolved into an Eden with rich, fertile soil that will grow any rose that can survive the hot, humid summers and cold winters of the Northeast and lower Midwest.

No, I didn't haul in truckloads of topsoil. Instead, I located a Long Island township that composts leaves and uses the compost for town parks and provides it free to residents, too. I also make some compost at home in a 3- by 4-foot bin. In addition to garden trimmings, I add weeds and kitchen scraps (no meat), as well as seaweed that I gather in the late summer. I also mix some seaweed with finished compost and use it as a winter mulch. A nearby National Park Police horse stable provides manure to any enterprising gardener who will haul it away; I bring the manure home in the fall and compost it over the winter for use in the spring.

Part of my garden is devoted to raising vegetables and berries. The more aesthetic and sensually satisfying portion of the garden is a rose bed along the front containing tea and miniature roses. Climbing roses border my garden: 'America' on an arbor against the garage and 'Cadenza' up on posts in the rear, with a cutting of 'Seven Sisters' in between. 'Golden Showers' and 'Sombreuil' are on an arbor along the driveway next to the neighbor's garage.

All of my roses get basically the same treatment—4 to 6 inches of compost and a generous helping of composted manure in spring, placed around the base of each plant. Along with this, I feed each plant bone meal, cottonseed meal and rock phosphate. I apply compost as a mulch in June or early July to help conserve moisture, keep the roots cool and keep down weeds and provide nutrients. No further feeding is done for the rest of the growing season. Compost with seaweed is applied as a winter mulch after the plants are dormant.

I use all-natural controls for insects and diseases in my vegetable garden, and treat my roses the same way. Japanese beetles and other voracious feeders seem to avoid this chemical-free environment, since it grows such healthy plants. When occasional clusters of aphids appear, I wash them away with a spray of water. I may have to repeat this procedure several days in a row until the aphids are gone. Aphids appear to be more of a problem if ants are farming them, so I control ants by applying borax in every hill.

Some roses develop blackspot during our hot and humid summers; damage is mild in some years, and quite severe in others. But by observing other rose gardens that have been on a rigorous spraying schedule, I've concluded that the damage from blackspot is no more severe in my no-spray garden than in gardens that have been repeatedly sprayed to "control" blackspot. When fall brings cooler weather, my roses recover and reward me with beautiful blooms.

Roses newly introduced to the garden, whether pot grown, transplants or bare root, take at least a season to become strong, disease- and insect-resistant plants. The impulse to give up on new plants is rather strong when they're infested with aphids or damaged by disease, especially when established plants next to them have no such problems. By the following season, though, these new plants are stronger and able to resist problems much more effectively.

I water my garden with a drip irrigation system. I've observed fewer problems with blackspot and mildew since installing this system several years ago.

Not having many plants of the same kind close together also seems to confuse insects and reduce their damage, some years to none. Insect eaters such as lady beetles, lacewings, spiders and many birds live in and around the garden, always on the ready for any meal that appears.

And so, although my cultivation methods are somewhat different from my grandmother's, I can smell the fragrance of the 'Seven Sisters' in my rose garden and savor the sweet berries, crisp carrots and tender red lettuce that she taught me to grow. My grandmother and now five of her daughters are gone, but 'Seven Sisters' and my beautiful garden remind me of them each day I kneel to pick a berry or smell the roses.

# EASY-CARE ROSES FOR THE
## NORTHEAST & LOWER MIDWEST

### Zones 5,8

**'Autumn Sunset'**
Shrub. Sport of 'Westerland'. Tall-growing, reaching 6' to 7', with spreading habit. Repeat blooming. Bears clusters of 2" blooms, blends of yellow, orange and pink. Very fragrant.

**'Viking Queen'**
Large-flowered climber. Lax canes, spreading habit, reaching 8' to 10'. Repeat bloomer. Fragrant, pink blooms with high centers are good for cutting.

**'Roundelay'**
Grandiflora. Upright growing, reaching 6' to 7'. Repeat blooming. Very fragrant dark crimson flowers open from a high pointed bud to a quartered form (as if cut into quarters) with tightly packed petals. Makes an excellent cut flower.

'VIKING QUEEN'

'AUTUMN SUNSET'

### 'Ma Perkins'

Floribunda. Bushy growth, reaching 4' to 5'. Repeat blooming. Clusters of salmon-pink flowers open immediately to a loose form, exposing the stamens. Light fragrance attracts honey bees.

### 'Cadenza'

Large-flowered climber. Stiff, upright habit, reaching 8' to 10'. Repeat bloomer. Bears long-stemmed clusters of velvety red flowers with light fragrance.

### 'Peace'

Hybrid tea. Upright growing, reaching 4' to 5'. Repeat-blooming flowers are yellow with hints of pink (in cooler weather, the pinker shades are more prominent). Flowers tend to be globular with densely packed petals, fragrant, on long stems.

'PEACE'

'CADENZA'

### 'Compassion'

Large-flowered climber. Lax canes, spreading habit, reaching 12' to 15'. Repeat bloomer. Apricot-pink, high-centered blooms are fragrant and good for cutting. Produces large, orange hips.

**'Fashion'**

Floribunda. Bushy growth reaching 4' to 5'. Repeat blooming. Large, loose-petaled coral blooms in clusters. Light fragrance.

**'America'**

Large-flowered climber. Stiff, arching habit, reaching 8' to 10'. Repeat bloomer. Long-stemmed, high-centered blooms are bright salmon, with strong fragrance.

**'Blaze'**

Large-flowered climber. Stiff, arching habit, reaching 8' to 10'. Repeat bloomer. Clusters of cupped-shaped, lightly fragrant red blooms.

**'Golden Showers'**

Large-flowered climber. Lax, arching habit, reaching 8' to 10'. Repeat bloomer. Clusters of golden-yellow, loosely petaled blooms are very fragrant. Produces large orange hips.

'GOLDEN SHOWERS'

'BLAZE'

**'TROPICANA'**

### 'Tropicana'
Hybrid tea. Upright growth reaching 6' to 7'. Repeat blooming. Large, orange-salmon blooms on long stems. Strong fragrance.

### 'Independence'
Floribunda. Height 4' to 5'; bushy growth. Repeat blooming. Tight, cupped-shaped orange-red blooms in clusters. Fragrant.

### 'Hawkeye Belle'
Shrub. Upright, stiff growth reaching 6' to 7'. Repeat blooming. Pale pink blooms on long stems have a slight fragrance. Good for cutting.

**'SOMBREUIL'**

### 'Sombreuil'
Climbing tea. Spreading, arching habit, reaching 12' to 15'. Repeat bloomer. Very fragrant white flowers with hints of pink and apricot. Large, globular buds open to flat, tightly petaled blooms on long stems.

# The Hardy Survivors

BY WILLENE B. CLARK

Surviving winter in the northeastern mountains is always a challenge—for roses *and* people. But while we gardeners winter by cozy woodstoves, our roses must endure long periods of often severe sub-zero cold (-20, -30, even -40° F) and then grow and bloom in rocky, thin topsoil and on sharply tilting contours.

In many respects, the needs of roses in cold climates (zones 3 to 5) are similar to those in more temperate regions: good soil preparation, care in planting and protection from disease. But harsh land and climate make unique demands, the most important of which is the careful selection of rose varieties.

The old garden rose types, along with a number of modern roses bred for hardiness, are the best performers in cold climates and high altitudes. Although many old garden roses have a limited bloom season, the spectacular quality of the show makes up for its brevity. Moreover, many are renowned for their fragrance and make handsome bushes after blooming.

When reading catalogues, don't be lulled by the notation "hardy"; try to determine the hardiness of the parentage of a rose before buying it. It's a good idea to ask local growers about a rose's performance in the area, since parentage is not always a reliable indicator of potential.

Almost all rugosas and their hybrids can take both the cold and rocky mountain soil, and as a bonus, need only a minimum of pruning and a rare spraying (never with commercial chemicals). Albas, damasks, gallicas, mosses and spinosissimas (or pimpinellifolias) require more pruning and usually some spraying, but are also tolerant of the mountain winter. Certain old garden types may not survive even with protection. On the other hand, a number of the species roses are wonderfully tough. Some of the roses hybridized by Buck, and a few of the polyanthas, floribundas and English varieties, will also make it through severe winters but require some protection to avoid winterkill of canes.

Among modern so-called bush roses, those of the Explorer group bred by Agriculture Canada are noted for hardiness, and many hybrids by Kordes of Germany, Meilland of France and Morden of Canada also endure a very harsh climate with aplomb. Most climbers and ramblers will not survive, or will not bloom in a very cold climate, but Canadian Explorer climbers and several by Kordes do well. The only climbers that are sufficiently vigorous in the mountains to adequately cover a full-sized arch are the species climbers (such as *R. rubiginosa*). Hybrid perpetuals, most floribundas and hybrid teas are iffy even with maximum protection. Fall-planted roses do much better in a cold-winter area than spring-planted ones, which often must struggle to catch up. Be prepared to wait four, or even five, years for many rose varieties to achieve their full potential. Transplant established bushes in the fall, too, and be prepared for a recovery period of about one year. Mountain soil can be very poor, so if you live at a high altitude be sure to condition the soil carefully. Dig down about 2 feet and remove any very rocky or shaly soil, or any hard-pan clay you encounter. Add a hefty shovelful of compost or rotted manure, and if the soil is very heavy, the same amount of moistened peat moss; add topsoil to replace any soil that was removed. Mountain soils tend to be acid, so you can also add a bit of lime—but remember that roses like their soil to be slightly acid.

When planting grafted roses in cold climates, be sure to protect the graft union (the bulge where the rootstock and graft are joined) by setting it 2 to 3 inches below ground surface. When you buy grafts, make sure a hardy rootstock was used. Consider making a special effort to obtain "own-root" roses—those grown from cuttings or seed, which tend to survive better than grafts. To avoid encouraging tender late growth, don't prune or fertilize mountain roses after the end of July.

With hard frosts, roses lose their leaves and become dormant. This is the time to prepare them for the long winter. Some roses need no special protection; put a shovelful or two of compost or composted manure on the crown of each. With a good snow cover, hardy roses will leaf-out in spring with little or no winter damage. In our area we wrap slightly sensitive roses with burlap, and for tender specimens, fill the cavities with shredded leaves or peat moss and tie a cord around the whole at several levels to secure the covering. A protected planting site in the lee of trees or on the south side of a building can eliminate the need for wrapping some borderline-hardy roses, such as Bourbons and Bucks.

Still tenderer roses, such as most floribundas, are cut back lightly when dormant and covered with a ventilated rose cap. We cut the hybrid teas back to about 14 inches and surround them with small-mesh wire cages filled with leaves and/or peat moss; they also require a protected, south-facing site. Except for the Explorers, we dismount all non-species climbers and wrap and tie them in burlap. We also brace broad composition board at an angle across the wrapped climber against the prevailing winds. Even with such protection, though, only the truly hardy climbers will perform well. A less-than-hardy rose might perform well for a year or two, then cease to bloom, or turn up its toes completely.

# EASY-CARE ROSES FOR COLD CLIMATES

## Zones 3-5

**'Hansa'**
Hybrid rugosa. Upright, spreading
habit, medium height. Freely suckering. Repeat blooming. Very fragrant
magenta blooms on short stems,
often in clusters.

'HANSA'

DOG ROSE

**Dog Rose** *(R. canina)*
Species. Stiff and arching habit,
reaching 8' to 10'. Non-repeating.
Pink, five-petaled blooms are borne
on short stems. Blooms are 1" to 2"
across, with light fragrance. Produces
bright orange hips.

**'Rose des Peintres'**
Centifolia. Spreading, lax growth
reaching 3' to 4' high. Non-repeating
bloomer. Produces large, globular,
pink blooms with tightly packed
petals. The weight of the blooms pulls
the canes down. Very fragrant.

R. SPINOSISSIMA ALTAICA

**'Autumn Damask'**
Damask. Medium-height shrub (to about 4') with a spreading habit. Bloom repeats in the autumn. Clusters of very fragrant pink flowers with 8 to 12 petals loosely formed. One of the oldest known cultivated roses.

**'Rose d'Amour'**
Species hybrid. Medium height (to 4'), freely suckering. Non-repeating. Pink, double-petaled blooms are fragrant. Possibly a naturally occurring hybrid of the native species, *Rosa virginiana*.

**R. spinosissima altaica**
Species. Moderate height, upright habit, suckering. Non-repeating. Very fragrant white blooms are 2" to 3" across, very short stems.

**'Old Pink Moss'**
Moss. Medium height, spreading habit, freely suckering. Pink, very double blooms are about 3" across. Has dense, mossy glands along pedicel. Very fragrant.

'OLD PINK MOSS'

# EASY-CARE ROSES FOR COLD CLIMATES

'CAREFREE BEAUTY'

**'Carefree Beauty'**
Shrub. Tall-growing, spreading habit, to 5' to 6' tall. Repeat bloomer. Large, lightly fragrant pink blooms are loosely formed with many petals. Produces orange hips.

**'Rose de Rescht'**
Portland. Medium height, spreading, freely suckering. Repeat blooming. Magenta, very double blooms, some in clusters, more often single stemmed. Very fragrant.

**'Alba Maxima'**
Alba. Stiff, upright habit, reaching 7' to 8'. Non-repeating bloomer. Produces creamy white, flat-shaped blooms 3" to 4" across, with wavy petals. Very fragrant.

'ALBA MAXIMA'

**'Eglantine Rose'**
**(R. rubiginosa)**
Species. Large-growing (to 10' to 12'), with arching canes. Non-repeating. Pink, five-petaled blooms on short stems. Although the bloom has little fragrance, the foliage has a strong apple scent. Produces bright orange hips.

### 'Complicata'

Species hybrid. Rambling habit; often grows up into trees. Non-repeating. Large, single-petaled, pink blooms are 3" to 4" across and have little fragrance. Produces large orange hips.

### 'Champlain'

Shrub. Medium height, spreading habit. Freely suckering. Repeat blooming. Clusters of lightly fragrant red blooms 2" to 3" across.

### 'Harison's Yellow'

Species hybrid. Large, spreading and freely suckering shrub. Non-repeating. Double, yellow blooms (1" across) on very short stems have a mild, unusual fragrance.

### Apothecary's Rose (R. gallica officinalis )

Gallica. Moderate height, spreading growth, freely suckering. Non-repeating. Very fragrant, red-pink, semi-double blooms are often borne in clusters. One of the oldest known cultivated roses. A striped sport of Apothecary's Rose is 'Rosa mundi' (*R. gallica versicolor* ).

APOTHECARY'S ROSE

'HARISON'S YELLOW'

# Baskets Full of Blooms

## A Rose Garden in the Deep South

BY IDA SHARP

**W**hen I started growing roses, my nostalgic visions of baskets full of blooms quickly gave way to the reality of our weather conditions in the deep South: mild winters, with short periods of freezing weather, moist springs both cool and warm, balmy hot summers with occasional drought and crisp autumns. Nearly perfect weather if you like the semi-tropics. Perfect conditions, too, for blackspot and other fungus diseases that thrive on moisture.

But after years of trying to grow modern hybrid teas that took gallons of chemicals and hours of work, I've found that I *can* have roses with a minimum of care. Most of these wonderful survivors are old garden roses, which are plagued

**Above: The sprawling rambler 'Dorothy Perkins' blooms once—but profusely.**

only by excessive growth brought on by our heat and moisture. Many of my favorite roses can still be found growing among the weeds in cemeteries, on abandoned homesites and in totally unexpected places. Some of them do fine on their own, unattended by human hands for years, undaunted by weeds and neglect.

In our warm climate, some of these roses bloom almost continuously from spring till frost and even later; it's not unusual to find their flowers on the table for New Year's Day. Many establish themselves quickly, and will soon look like they've been there for generations. Most are extremely disease and insect free.

My favorite choice so far is 'Mrs. B. R. Cant'. If I could have but one rose in my garden, it would be this early tea rose—one of the types often found in Victorian paintings. *Nothing* is impossible with 'Mrs. B. R. Cant'; in one year I had a 10-inch plant grow to 4 feet. It will provide you with an abundance of blossoms for bouquets with little effort. Competing for my favor with the other easy-care roses in my garden is 'Duchesse de Brabant'. With its flowers of purely pink perfection and noticeable fragrance, this rose will undoubtedly establish itself as a contender for your favorite, just as it did with Theodore Roosevelt.

In my experience, there are no modern hybrid teas that can truthfully be considered carefree for our area. Most require at least some application of chemicals to ward off disease; others require regular weekly spraying of fungicides. But there are enough truly carefree selections that modern gardeners can successfully grow and fulfill their dreams of baskets of roses.

# A Southeast Coastal Rose Garden

### BY RUTH KNOPF

I grew my first old roses in upstate South Carolina, in a former cotton field. I began that garden of old roses with plants rooted from cuttings given to me by a friend, who also taught me to root roses in a washtub.

There was no plan for the garden. It featured the plants, not the design. But it was a wonderful and surprisingly beautiful creation. Most of the roses I grew there were found in South Carolina and the Southeast. Without knowing it, I chose the best roses for my situation and garden. These beauties were survivors of old plantings in the past. They had already stood the tests of time—extreme hot and cold temperatures, high humidity, drought and hurricanes, as well as our ordinary weather. They endured while many other roses disappeared. This was truly survival of the fittest.

I was fortunate that most classes of roses did well for me in this garden, which was in zone 7 and 700 feet above sea level, with sandy clay soil. Then, in 1990, my husband died and I moved 200 miles south on the South Carolina coast and began all over again.

My second garden began with knowledge of the old roses I'd grown, but not of the new, warmer climate and sandier soil. After three years I find that most of the roses that perform best here are those from the warm regions of China. The Chinas, teas, Noisettes, banksias and musks seem to do best. Though not as old, the hybrid musks, ramblers and the hybrid Chinas also do well. Most of the roses found in this area are grown on their own roots, and so are those in my garden. I'm also experimenting with some roses budded on *Rosa fortuniana,* a prolific plant from China, as the rootstock; so far this seems to give strength to weaker roses, but time will tell.

The problem of contending with many very invasive weeds and grasses has also been new to me. It's necessary to maintain control from the start of the making of a flower bed; later is too late. It's also important to plant well, by digging a large hole and mixing manure and peat moss with the existing soil. Fall is our best time to plant.

In my upstate garden, I fertilized only once a year, and I did not use high-nitrogen chemical fertilizers. Roses treated this way build up strong growth over time, and are more disease and insect resistant. In my coastal garden with such sandy soil, fertilizing more often is necessary. Water is also important, and I find that PVC pipe used in the rose beds with a hole drilled at each bush works well and is economical. The piping is covered with landscape fabric or black plastic and then a heavy mulch of locally available chipped bark. This really conserves moisture in our very hot summers. In the intense heat of the coastal area, I find some roses actually do better in partial shade.

I do not spray. Most of these roses came along before chemical sprays were developed, and still they endured. The key is choosing the types that are most disease resistant in your area. I wonder why we expect perfection in roses anyway—do we make the same demands of other plants?

Over the years the old tea roses, a class that originated in China, have probably become my favorites—unusually large, graceful bushes with frequently prolific and elegant blooms. They take the prize for being most disease resistant. Most are pastel in color with some in deeper shades of pink and red. I find these roses everywhere throughout the Southeast, and they are to me truly roses of our southern heritage.

## Zones 7-9

### 'Tausendschön'

Rambler. Large, sprawling shrub with lax, thornless canes reaching to 15'. Non-repeat bloomer. Produces large clusters of wavy-petaled blooms in various shades of pink to white. No fragrance.

'TAUSENDSCHÖN'

'MUTABILIS'

### 'Mutabilis'

China. Large, spreading shrub grows to 5' to 6'. Repeat bloomer. Single-petaled, lightly fragrant blooms are about 2" across and change from straw yellow to vivid scarlet before dropping off the plant.

### 'Baronne Henriette de Snoy'

Tea. Large, spreading shrub. Repeat bloomer. Fragrant, large, pointed buds open to salmon-pink with flushes of red-pink.

**'Maman Cochet'**
Tea. Medium height (to about 4'). Repeat blooming. Large, pointed, red-tinged buds open to porcelain pink blooms that are very full and double, with a sweet fragrance.

**'The Fairy'**
Polyantha. Spreading habit, grows to 4' high and wide. Repeat blooming. Produces clusters of small, multiple-petaled pink blossoms with no fragrance.

**'Dorothy Perkins'**
Rambler. Sprawling habit, 15' to 20' high. Non-repeating. Produces large clusters of small, light- to medium-pink flowers with no fragrance.

**'Monsieur Tillier'**
Tea. Medium to tall, averaging about 5'. Repeat blooming. Densely petaled blooms are combinations of red, pink and shades of orange. Fragrant.

'THE FAIRY'

'MAMAN COCHET'

'CLOTHILDE SOUPERT'

### 'Cl. Mrs. Herbert Stevens'

Climbing hybrid tea. Sprawling, vigorous plant. Repeat bloomer. Long, pointed buds open to white, high-centered, multi-petaled blooms. Flowers tend to nod from weight. Fragrant.

### 'Vanity'

Hybrid musk. Large, sprawling shrub, with some canes reaching up to 15'. Repeat bloomer. Produces large clusters of large, five-petaled red-pink blooms. Light fragrance.

### 'Clotilde Soupert'

Polyantha. Low to medium height (2' to 5'), with spreading habit. Repeat blooming. Very fragrant, tightly packed petals are pale pink fading to white and tend to have a cupped shape. Flowers may ball up and fail to open.

### 'Alister Stella Gray'

Noisette. Large, sprawling plant. Repeat blooming. Large, multi-petaled yellow flowers fade to white. Clusters of fragrant flowers.

'ALISTER STELLA GRAY'

'SAFRANO'

'BELINDA'

### 'Bon Silène'
Tea. Large, spreading shrub, 4' to 5' high. Repeat bloomer. Fragrant, bright pink, loosely double blooms.

### 'Belinda'
Hybrid musk. Large, sprawling shrub grows to 8' to 10'. Repeat blooming. Produces large clusters of small, five-petaled pink blooms. No fragrance.

### 'Safrano'
Tea. Reaches 8' tall and wide if left unpruned. Repeat bloomer. Loose, fragrant, apricot-buff flowers.

### 'Marie Van Houtte'
Tea. Large, spreading shrub grows to 4' to 5'. Repeat bloomer. Large, fragrant, cream-yellow blooms are flushed with pink in cool weather.

# Desert Roses

BY MIKE SHOUP

T exas is a conglomeration of climates. In southeast Texas—south of a line from Fort Worth to San Antonio—the weather is characterized by high humidity with extremes of summer heat and winter cold. This, along with diverse soil types, yields conditions that only the strongest of roses can conquer—the same roses that thrive in other parts of the South (see page 65).

The hot and arid climate of far west and northern Texas (including areas from Lubbock to Amarillo, and westward to the Guadalupe Mountains and Big Bend) and the southwestern states is more conducive to growing roses, since the diseases associated with high humidity aren't a problem. There the key is proper irrigation. The type of irrigation isn't important, but timing is: Water roses deeply and avoid watering in the middle of the day. Not only is the irrigation less efficient then, but excessive evaporation leaves residues of salt that may be damaging.

The best varieties for Texas and the Southwest are often the old garden roses still surviving in abandoned homesites or forgotten cemeteries. Among these roses are a few gems that are very fragrant, repeating their bloom often through the year, with very showy flowers. They're resilient enough to tolerate the tough Texas climates as far west as El Paso and into parts of New Mexico and Arizona—zones 7 and 8—even without human care. The colder regions of the Southwest require the hardier varieties recommended on pages 59 to 64.

China's greatest gift to man isn't the printing press or gunpowder—but rather repeat-blooming roses that have since lent their genes to modern roses, giving them the same remontancy. Two of the classes from China, the Chinas and teas, are extremely floriferous in Texas and the Southwest, have a spicy or fresh fragrance and are seldom bothered by pests or diseases. Occasional blackspot and mildew haven't debilitated established plants.

The China rose 'Old Blush' is pink with darker tones (giving it its name). 'Mutabilis' is known as the butterfly rose because when in bloom (which is often), it mimics the look of butterflies dancing around its thick foliage. Yellow, orange, pink and red are all found within its single flowers. 'Louis Philippe' is one

'Archduke Charles'. The Chinas and teas are extremely floriferous in Texas and the Southwest, have a spicy or fresh fragrance and are seldom bothered by pests.

of the best red Chinas, and is also steeped in history: Lorenzo de Zavala, as Texas's first minister to France, brought it back from Europe in 1834 to adorn his homestead in Lynchburg, Texas. Tea roses can be more ornate than the Chinas, with larger blossoms and a wider range of colors.

The South can tout another group of roses as its own: The Noisettes—bred by John Champneys, a rice farmer in Charleston—are also perfect for our Texas and Southwestern heat. All are great repeat-blooming climbing roses. The flowers are borne in clusters and have outstanding fragrance. Best of all is the soft, romantic quality that they bring to a garden, with their cascading effect on fences and arbors.

A few of the species roses deserve recommendation for gardeners in the Lone Star State and the Southwest. These are traffic stoppers in the spring with their intense bloom, and they provide foliage interest through the summer. They're vigorous beyond comprehension, occasionally growing 20 feet a year— the perfect choice for covering a fence or naturalizing your yard.

### Zones 7 and warmer
#### (a few will work in Zone 6)

'OLD BLUSH'

**'Old Blush'**
China. Medium-sized shrub (to 4' to 6' high). Repeat bloomer. Loose-shaped blooms are pink with darker tones, lightly fragrant.

**'Mrs. B. R. Cant'**
Tea. Grows to 8'; can be trained into tree form. Repeat blooming. Fragrant, deeply quartered blooms are reddish pink and silvery pink.

**'Duchesse de Brabant'**
Tea. Large, spreading shrub (to 5' to 7' high). Repeat blooming. Tulip-shaped pink blooms have a strong fragrance. A white sport, 'Mrs. Joseph Schwartz', is equally impressive.

'MRS. B. R. CANT'

'CHEROKEE'

### 'Mrs. Dudley Cross'
Tea. Large, spreading shrub, to 5' to 7' high. Repeat blooming. Fragrant blooms are a distinctive, muted yellow-pink. No thorns.

### 'Céline Forestier'
Noisette. Tall growing, with an upright habit, reaching up to 15'. Repeat blooming. Fragrant, quartered blooms are yellow with faint shades of apricot.

### 'Cherokee'
Species. Very vigorous, spreading, mounding shrub, reaching over 15'. Non-repeat bloomer. Fragrant, large, single-petaled white flowers.

### 'Archduke Charles'
Tea. Medium-sized shrub (4' to 5' high). Repeat blooming. Large, high-centered blooms are rich crimson with distinct shades of pink. Fragrant.

'CÉLINE FORESTIER'

# EASY-CARE ROSES FOR TEXAS & THE SOUTHWEST

**'Louis Philippe'**
China. Medium-sized shrub (5' to 6' high). Repeat blooming. Full, crimson-rose, globular blooms average 3" across. Light, fruity fragrance.

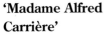

'LOUIS PHILIPPE'

**'Lamarque'**
Noisette. Tall-growing, sprawling shrub, reaching as high as 15'. Repeat blooming. Fragrant, ivory blooms are flat and multi-petaled.

**'Jaune Desprez'**
Noisette. Tall-growing, sprawling shrub, reaching over 15'. Repeat blooming. Large, cupped blossoms of pink have strong flushes of yellow. Fragrant.

'JAUNE DESPREZ'

**'Madame Alfred Carrière'**
Noisette. Tall-growing, more upright than sprawling, reaching over 15'. Repeat blooming. Large, cupped blooms are creamy white with hints of pink flushes. Strong fragrance. Has been known to bloom in the winter.

### 'Fortuniana'
Species hybrid. Vigorous, spreading plant with long canes reaching over 20'. Non-repeat bloomer. 2"-wide, white, multi-petaled flowers have a light fragrance.

### 'Lady Banks' Rose'
### (Rosa banksiae banksiae)
Species. Very vigorous, tall-growing and spreading shrub reaching well over 20'. Non-repeat bloomer. Small, white, multi-petaled flowers. Fragrant.

### 'Mermaid'
Species hybrid. Very vigorous, sprawling, easily reaching over 20' with long, arching canes. Repeat blooming. Large, single-petaled yellow flowers, 4" to 5" across. Fruity fragrance.

'MERMAID'

'SOUVENIR DE LA MALMAISON'

### 'Souvenir de la Malmaison'
Bourbon. Medium-sized, spreading shrub, reaching 3' to 4' high. Repeat blooming. Light pink, very double flowers, often with a button eye or a classic quartered shape. Very fragrant.

# Floriferous in Seattle

### BY JOHN CLEMENTS

The western part of the northwestern U.S. has a maritime climate similar to that of England. West of the Cascade Mountains in Oregon, Washington and British Columbia, the weather is tempered by the warming effects of the Japanese current. Rain is frequent, though generally light, from November through early June. Our 40 inches of rain per year is about the same as that in New York City and London (although immediate coastal areas may receive nearly double the rainfall). Our summers are generally dry, with only about one day of rain per month. East of the Cascade Mountains it's a different story. Due to the rain shadow cast by the mountains, the climate is near desert-like, with around 10 inches of rain a year. Winter temperatures can drop to 20 degrees below zero during severe periods, which means that less-hardy rose varieties (such as the hybrid teas and floribundas) need winter protection.

West of the Cascades are found the same rose diseases prevalent in other moist climates, though not nearly as severe. In the spring and fall, powdery mildew may at times disfigure rosebuds, but does no permanent damage to the bush. Blackspot may affect the lower leaves of many varieties, but it only slightly disfigures the bush and again does no permanent damage. Although it's seen in some gardens, rust is somewhat rare, and is really only a problem on hybrid perpetuals and a few other roses. East of the Cascades, some mildew may be present, but blackspot and rust are very rare.

All in all, you can grow and enjoy roses in the Northwest without spraying with chemical preparations, especially if you're willing to settle for a little less than perfection. You can control fungus diseases by watering with a drip system or, if using overhead watering, by doing so only in the early morning so that the foliage dries before nightfall, since that's when most fungi grow and prosper. Insect problems in the region include the usual aphids and spider mites, which can be lived with as they do no permanent damage. Aphids are a problem here

The showy 'Oranges and Lemons'. The climate and soils west of the Cascades are ideal for growing large rose bushes and lush, beautiful blooms.

only for a short period in May or June. You can control them by hosing them off with a strong spray of water, or removing them by hand. Spider mites may appear during hot, dry weather; you can partially control these by using a water wand to spray water on the underside of the lower leaves.

In colder areas, budded roses will need extra protection. Own-root roses survive the cold much better, and are also more likely to be free of virus diseases.

Our northwestern soils are as varied as our terrain. Areas west of the Cascades generally have a clay soil that at times is described by gardeners as "little sticky," "big sticky" or "damn sticky," according to how much of it collects on your shoes. The soil needs good drainage. Plant your rose in a large hole—2 feet across by 2 feet deep. Add manure in the bottom of the hole to a depth of about 6 inches, and refill the hole with a mixture of half existing soil and half compost. All in all, the climate and soils west of the Cascades are some of the world's most ideal for growing large rose bushes and lush, beautiful blooms.

# EASY-CARE ROSES FOR THE NORTHWEST

## Zones 6-8

THE CLIMBING FORM OF 'CÉCILE BRÜNNER'

'CONSTANCE SPRY'

**'Cécile Brünner'**
Polyantha. Reaches 2' tall. Repeat blooming. Small, delicate pink, double blooms have light fragrance.

**'Royal Blush'**
Shrub. Tall-growing, up to 6'. Non-repeat bloomer. Fully double, quartered blooms of soft pink. Very fragrant. New cultivar from Germany.

**'Constance Spry'**
Shrub. Large, arching canes, reaching 7' high. Non-repeat bloomer. Large, double, cupped blooms are clear pink. Strong fragrance.

**'Oranges and Lemons'**
Shrub. Upright, spreading habit, reaching up to 6'. Fully double blooms of bright orange and yellow stripes. Fragrant.

# EASY-CARE ROSES FOR THE NORTHWEST

**'Altissimo'**
Large-flowered climber. Stiff, upright growth, reaching 6' to 9'. Repeat blooming. Large, 5-petaled, single blooms are a rich, velvety blood-red. Light fragrance.

**'Sally Holmes'**
Shrub. Vigorous, upright growth, reaching 8' to 10'. Repeat bloomer. Huge trusses of soft-apricot buds open to white single blooms. Light fragrance.

**'Westerland'**
Shrub. Tall-growing, spreading habit, reaching 6' to 8' high. Repeat bloomer. Ruffled blooms of apricot-copper and orange blends. Fragrant.

'SALLY HOLMES'

'WESTERLAND'

**'L.D. Braithwaite'**
Shrub. Spreading, upright growth, reaching 5'. Repeat bloomer. Fragrant, fully double blooms are rich crimson-red.

'JEANNE LAJOIE'

### 'Jeanne Lajoie'
Climbing miniature. Spreading growth with canes reaching 5' to 7'. Repeat blooming. A profusion of small, perfectly formed hybrid-tea-shaped blooms of marshmallow pink. No fragrance.

### 'Queen Margrethe'
Shrub. Medium-sized with spreading growth, reaching 3' high. Repeat bloomer. Fully double 3" blooms are pink and very fragrant.

### 'Charles Albanel'
Hybrid rugosa. Low, spreading growth, averaging 2' high. Repeat bloomer. Very fragrant, red-purple, semi-double blooms.

### 'Dapple Dawn'
Shrub. Reaches 5' tall. Repeat blooming. Large, gossamer-pink, single blooms. Fragrant.

'DAPPLE DAWN'

# EASY-CARE ROSES FOR THE NORTHWEST

**'Thérèse Bugnet'**
Hybrid rugosa. Tall, upright shrub, reaching over 7'. Repeat blooming. Ruffled double blooms are soft lilac-pink and fragrant.

**'Dortmund'**
Large-flowered climber. Reaches 7' to 10' tall. Repeat bloomer. Medium-sized, semi-double blooms are bright, scarlet-red with white centers. No fragrance. Produces beautiful display of orange hips in the fall.

**'Alba Semi-plena'**
Alba. Upright growth to 6' or 7'. Non-repeat bloomer. Semi-double, pure white blooms with golden centers. Fragrant. Produces scarlet hips.

'ALBA SEMI-PLENA'

'DORTMUND'

# A Rose Enthusiast's Paradise

BY PHILLIP ROBINSON

California is often described as a rose enthusiast's paradise, where the roses grow to perfection, to giant proportions and with total neglect. This is simplistic, at best, since it's almost as difficult to be specific about rose culture for this single state as it would be for all the other states combined. The climate varies from the cool, foggy coast to hot central valleys, even hotter and drier deserts, and finally to the higher elevations with their cold winters. The term microclimate is often used in California. Growing conditions can change radically in a few miles due to the interaction of a myriad of topographic, continental, oceanic and latitudinal factors.

Soils also vary wildly within California. Generally the areas with high winter rainfall in the northern parts of the state have soils on the acid side, varying with the geological underpinnings. As you move to the drier inland and southern areas, soils tend to be alkaline and require the use of sulfur and/or acid fertilizer and plenty of organic materials to help buffer the pH. Irrigation water is often also alkaline, compounding the problem.

All in all, though, the conditions here are very favorable to rose culture, including the cultivation of almost any cultivar or species available—many of them without spraying. The mild winters don't necessitate winter protection of roses, and a long growing season produces large, robust, floriferous bushes. Irrigation is required, since summer rainfall is almost unknown in most of the state. These dry summers make blackspot a rare occurrence. The most common disease is powdery mildew, especially in areas of ocean influence. Rust is also prevalent, but can be greatly reduced with proper rose selection and with hygiene and dormant sprays with a copper fungicide. Recently downy mildew has become a problem in our cool, damp spring and fall weather. In certain seasons thrips, mites or aphids can be troublesome, but can be controlled with a variety of non-toxic methods (see page 36).

It's well worth experimenting with different types and varieties of roses. Disease resistance and performance can vary widely by region and season; a variety that is completely clean in one area can be a poor risk in another. Just be observant and open to new types and you can have a beautiful and diverse garden. Since selection is key to avoiding disease and pests, here's a quick run-down of some roses that are most and least susceptible in California:

🌹 Most of the gallica roses are free from rust, but some (notably 'Belle de Crecy') do mildew badly on occasion.

🌹 All of the true alba roses are completely free from disease here in California. The rust they're susceptible to in England doesn't seem to be present here.

🌹 Unfortunately, the true centifolias are all magnets for rust in my garden, though they seem free of mildew.

🌹 As a group, the tea roses are quite rust resistant; 'Homère' is the one exception. Mildew is possible, especially in coastal gardens or in very foggy seasons

**The mild winters—and therefore long growing season—throughout much of California enable gardeners to grow large, robust and floriferous bushes.**

inland, but otherwise the teas are tough and reliable all-season producers of pastel blossoms.

🌹 Few of the hybrid perpetuals have much resistance to disease, but some of the early varieties and some of the closely related Portland roses can be relied upon.

🌹 Almost all of the hybrid musks are disease resistant and shade tolerant. 🌹

# EASY-CARE ROSES FOR CALIFORNIA

## Zones 6-9

**'Coquette des Blanches'**
Bourbon. Medium to tall growth, upright and spreading. Repeat bloomer. White, loosely cupped blooms are flushed with pink. Fragrant.

**'Étoile de Lyon'**
Tea. Medium-sized, with spreading growth. Repeat bloomer. Large, full, quartered yellow flowers. Fragrant.

**'Nouveau Vulcain'**
Gallica. Medium height, with spreading habit. Non-repeat bloomer. Sumptuous, maroon-purple blooms are very fragrant.

**'Adam Messerich'**
Bourbon. Large, upright plant. Repeat bloomer. Clusters of loosely petaled carmine-rose flowers. Fragrant.

'COQUETTE DES BLANCHES'

'ADAM MESSERICH'

### 'Blanche de Belgique'

Alba. Vigorous, upright growth, reaching to 6'. Non-repeat bloomer. Full, globular, pure-white flowers have a strong fragrance.

'BLANCHE DE BELGIQUE'

### 'Blairii No. 2'

Hybrid China. Very vigorous growth, with spreading habit. Long canes reach 8' to 10'. Non-repeat bloomer. Two-toned pink, cupped, multi-petaled flowers. Fragrant.

### "Spice"

Tea. Large, spreading habit. Repeat bloomer. Flowers are very pale pink, nearly white, loosely petaled with a spicy, grapefruit-like fragrance. Discovered and named by old-rose enthusiasts in Bermuda.

### 'Clytemnestra'

Hybrid musk. Very vigorous, spreading shrub. Repeat bloomer. Small, loosely petaled apricot-pink flowers. Fragrant.

'CLYTEMNESTRA'

**'GRANNY GRIMMETTS'**

**'MARÉCHAL NIEL'**

**'Granny Grimmetts'**
Hybrid perpetual. Medium-growth habit, bushy. Repeat bloomer. Crimson-mauve, fully petaled, cupped flowers, strong fragrance.

**'Comtesse du Cayla'**
China. Medium-sized, upright shrub. Repeat bloomer. Nasturtium-colored, loosely formed flowers. Fragrant.

**'Maréchal Niel'**
Noisette. Tall, vigorous climber, reaching to 15'. Repeat bloomer. Golden-yellow, bell-shaped flowers are intensely fragrant.

### 'La Rubanée'

Gallica. Medium height, with spreading growth. Non-repeat bloomer. Large, cupped blooms have crimson-purple tones on blush white. Very fragrant. Also known as 'Village Maid'.

'LA RUBANÉE'

### 'Marchesa Boccella'

Hybrid perpetual. Medium to tall, spreading shrub. Repeat bloomer. Tightly packed magenta-pink flowers, often with a button eye. Fragrant. Has long masqueraded as 'Jacques Cartier'.

### 'Mousseline'

Moss. Medium height, spreading habit. Repeat bloomer. White, loosely petaled blooms tinged with pink. Fragrant. Often sold as 'Alfred de Dalmas'.

### 'Blush Noisette'

Noisette. Medium to tall shrub, sometimes a climber. Soft-pink, multi-petaled flowers in large clusters. Fragrant.

'BLUSH NOISETTE'

# A Strong-willed Orchestra

BY JIM JOANNIDES

JUST OFF A BARREN, heavily trafficked intersection on the Bowery in New York City, there is a restful sight—a long, narrow, green snake of a garden. This garden—loosely managed, community-style—is just over 20 years old, one of the first of its kind in Manhattan. It sits over the subway line, and all the stepping stones vibrate whenever the "F" train passes underneath.

The soil in this garden is a totally local product: sand and crushed brick of collapsed buildings, rotted leaves from the Old Marble Cemetery, spent hops from the Manhattan Brewery in SoHo and small amounts of sawdust from a cabinetmaker's shop. In terms of drainage, the soil is a rock gardener's dream: fast and clean. At the end of the garden that's most exposed to traffic noise, ozone and the bad vibes of a populace at odds with itself is our rose plot.

All gardens tend to shape themselves, and the gardener stands before his or her own garden like the guest conductor before a strong-willed orchestra only pretending to be following. After a series of failures with space-hogging, shade-producing Bourbons and hybrid perpetuals that would not "perpetuate," our inventory of roses shifted to the smaller gallicas (in the area that gets adequate sun only in June) and to the good Portlands and the delightful teas (the saxophones, clarinets and violins of the rose plot). These roses grow alongside nice haze-blue thickets of old cottage pinks; short, fat blades of irises; oil-green tufts of *Coreopsis* 'Moonbeam'; pin-cushion scabiosas and thimble-form, electric-blue eryngiums. All of these mix so freely that any hierarchical notion of underplanting is pretty much null and void (as is proper in a community garden). There are no prima donna roses, no great formal statements. But the rose plot does have its overall subtle charm, and tea roses have had a quiet hand in this.

Teas are, of course, the predecessors of the hybrid teas. Their flowers are loosely globular or cupped or petticoat ruffled, and unlike hybrid teas, which were bred for bud shape and large size, every stage of the tea's inflorescence has a fascinating new twist or charming variation. They are scented with a thick, fruity perfume. Tea roses went out of fashion because of their soft color—salmon pinks, pale yellows and creamy whites—and the tendency of their blossoms to gracefully nod and flop onto other plants. ("Isn't there anything you can do with them—stake them or something?" one visitor cried in great alarm.)

Tea roses seem to like sandy soil, and in Manhattan they bloom frequently all summer. The leaves are like those of a nandina or bamboo, with a transparent effect; they dapple rather than shade the ground. And they tend to grow horizontally rather than making great upward shoots. In New York City they don't grow

At the end of a Manhattan community garden that's most exposed to traffic noise, ozone and the bad vibes of a populace at odds with itself is the rose plot.

large, because they freeze back to where they're covered each winter.

The great oven of Manhattan's summer, and the lettuce-soup feeling of its foul air, brings out these characteristics in old, non-tea roses:

🌹 Any shy-to-repeat rose becomes even shier. (The much-loved 'La Reine Victoria' doesn't rebloom at all for us here.)

🌹 The life cycle of a blossom is sped up drastically, into a sort of hysteria.

🌹 Likewise, blossom form is often skimped on; doubles become semi-doubles, quartering blossoms become muddled and so on.

🌹 Rich reds and purples often come out a harsh, empty red-magenta, while pinks lose their subtle rose, coral or lilac component.

🌹 Fragrance takes something of a nosedive.

We fertilize lightly here in the belief that a continuous supply of small amounts of nutrients from well dug-in compost, weak solutions of fish emulsion and top dressings of beer hops are better than monthly jolts of high-numbered fertilizers. Stronger dressings of an organic rose food are applied in April and again two or three weeks after the major bloom, allowing each plant a little period of sulky recuperation. Based perhaps on the shaky proposition that life in Manhattan is three times as intense and satisfying as that lived elsewhere, our local nurseries charge roughly triple what garden-supply centers do in the suburbs, and this figures into many of our economies. 🌹

# EASY-CARE ROSES FOR THE INNER CITY

## Zones 6-9

**'Cardinal de Richelieu'**
Gallica. Medium-height, spreading shrub. Non-repeat bloomer. Unique chocolate-purple flowers, lightly fragrant.

**'Comte de Chambord'**
Portland. Medium-growth habit, reaches to 3'. Spreading shrub can be pegged for compactness. Repeat bloomer. Very fragrant, large, quartered flowers packed with deep lilac-pink petals. Color stands up well to heat.

**'Mrs. Herbert Stevens'**
Hybrid tea. Medium height, with bushy growth habit. Repeat bloomer. Unusual, nodding, white flowers look something like pinwheels. Light fragrance.

'CARDINAL DE RICHELIEU'

'MRS. HERBERT STEVENS'

# EASY-CARE ROSES FOR THE INNER CITY

**'Rose du Roi'**
Portland. Medium height, upright and spreading habit. Repeat bloomer. Fully petaled blooms have wine-red centers and slate purple outer petals. Strong fragrance.

'GLOIRE DE DIJON'

'ROSE DU ROI'

**'Gloire de Dijon'**
Tea. Tall, climbing habit. Repeat bloomer. Large, globular flowers are apricot to soft yellow. Strong fragrance.

**'Merveille de Lyon'**
Hybrid perpetual. Medium to tall habit, with long canes reaching to 5'. Once-bloomer with sparse repeat. Large, cupped, white flowers. Light fragrance.

**'Belle de Crécy'**
Gallica. Medium-height, spreading shrub. Non-repeat bloomer. Flat, tightly petaled, quartered flowers are deep pink tarnishing to indigo, very fragrant. Holds color well in heat. Tolerant of half-day shade.

# EASY-CARE ROSES FOR THE INNER CITY

**'The Reeve'**
Shrub. Upright, large-growing shrub. Repeat bloomer. Large, globular, fully petaled pink flowers. Strong fragrance.

**'Vershuren'**
Hybrid tea. Medium, upright growth. Repeat bloomer. Globular, multi-petaled, clear-pink blooms. Strong fragrance. Unique, variegated foliage.

'THE REEVE'

**'The Yeoman'**
Shrub. Medium height, upright habit. Repeat bloomer. Loosely cupped, flat, translucent yellow-orange petals. Strong myrrh fragrance.

**'Boule de Neige'**
Bourbon. Graceful, spreading habit. Repeat bloomer. Fully petaled, globular, white flowers. Strong fragrance.

'BOULE DE NEIGE'

**'Lavender Pinocchio'**
Floribunda. Low height, spreading habit. Repeat bloomer. Wavy-petaled blooms with unusual russet-lavender color. Light fragrance.

**'Mme. Mélanie Willermoz'**
Tea. Medium height, compact, graceful habit. Repeat bloomer. Small, nodding, fully petaled, ruffled white flowers with tinges of pink. Strong, fruity fragrance.

**'Mme. Legras de St. Germain'**
Alba. Spreading, vigorous habit, medium height. Long canes with no prickles. Shade tolerant. Non-repeat bloomer. Very double, flat, white flowers. Strong fragrance.

'MME. LEGRAS DE ST. GERMAIN'

'FÉLICITÉ PARMENTIER'

**'Félicité Parmentier'**
Alba. Low, upright, spreading habit. Shade tolerant. Non-repeat bloomer. Flat, multi-petaled, cream-white flowers. Strong fragrance.

# OUR
# ROSY FUTURE

### Rose breeders are working to develop new roses with lots of color for a lot less work

BY TOM CARRUTH

OMETIMES WHEN YOU gaze into the crystal ball of the rose world, the image seems a little fuzzy. But one picture of our rosy future that comes through clearly is the continuing expansion of the shrub rose class—landscape roses that give gardeners just what they want: lots of color for less work.

Of course, the notion of what constitutes the "perfect" rose will vary widely from person to person, but to me the ideal shrub rose should not only bloom profusely and repeat quickly, but also naturally resist the major fungal diseases, be hardy in most climates, not require pruning (just occasional shaping), and have an attractive usable habit with abundant foliage.

Of course, in this perfect rose for a perfect world, a glorious fragrance would be the icing on the cake.

There's still lots of room for variety in my definition of the ideal landscape rose—for all differing flower forms and sizes, from miniature to monster, single to ruffled, quartered or quilled. There's room, too, for all sorts of growth habits—groundcovers, spilling fountains, rounded masses or tall sentinels. And when it comes to color, anything goes.

The European breeders are far and away ahead of the pack when it comes to developing these new landscape roses. For instance, the Kordes family in Germany produced an unassuming white floribunda back in 1958 called 'Iceberg', which has risen to become one of the most commonly used roses in the landscape and one of the top ten roses of the world—a remarkable feat since the rose was never marketed or patented in the United States. Among the many jewels

One thing about the roses of the near future is clear: There will be more and more shrub roses—landscape roses that provide lots of color for little work. The 'Bonica' shrub rose above is hardy, disease resistant and blooms all summer long.

still to come from Kordes, look for some great groundcovers (such as the white 'Jeepers Creepers') and several new rugosa hybrids.

Meilland in France has aggressively marketed shrub roses with the Meidiland series—a group of mostly groundcover types. Meilland's 'Bonica' was the first shrub rose to capture the All-America Rose Selection (AARS) award, in 1987. Meilland continues to dominate the AARS shrub category with two more winners, 'Carefree Wonder' (1991) and 'Carefree Delight' (1996).

A breeder from the Netherlands, Peter Ilsink of Interplant Nurseries, has also stunned the rose world with some spectacular new shrub roses. There's 'Eyeopener' (first of the red groundcovers), 'Lavender Dream' (a spilling fountain of clustered lavender flowers) and 'Lady of the Dawn' (a mountainous mass of blushed cream blossoms). Peter's roses have scooped up awards from around the world. Soon to come will be some gorgeous groundcovers and patios in clear yellow—a rare color among shrub roses.

The first floribundas came to us around the turn of the century from Poulsen Roser in Denmark. Pernille Poulsen-Olsen and her husband Mogens have carried on the family tradition very well with some wonderful shrub roses. Young's American Roses is about to market a whole line of Poulsen varieties called the Town & Country series. 'Queen Margrethe' captures the old rose style on a compact, free-blooming plant with great disease resistance.

Some of the very best floribundas continue to translate well into usage as landscape roses. Sam McGredy's 'Sexy Rexy' is a perfect example, with its masses of ruffled pink blossoms set against the great shiny clean foliage that typifies his bloodlines. From the late Jack Harkness of England will come the 1996 AARS-winning floribunda called 'Livin' Easy', with its clusters of apricot-orange flowers, loads of glossy green leaves and some of the best blackspot resistance yet.

The Dickson family in Ireland were instrumental in marketing patio roses in Europe. In our climate they become mini-shrubs (for lack of a better term) with small flowers and foliage carried in great abundance on fairly large, very clean plants. Two English neighbors, Gareth Fryer and Chris Warner, will be adding their own contributions to this unusual category soon.

Now don't get the impression that the U.S. breeders have been resting on their laurels. After all, Denny Morey's 'Temple Bells' has been used to breed almost all the groundcover roses coming from Europe. The late Bill Warriner produced a floribunda from 'Iceberg' that was the first successfully mass-marketed shrub rose in the U.S. It's called 'Simplicity'. Both a white and red version have since been produced, but haven't met with as much success. Warriner and his young partner, Keith Zary (the current breeder for Jackson & Perkins) share

'Iceberg', a floribunda, against a background of *Daphne burkwoodii* 'Carol Mackie'. Some of the best easy-care roses on the horizon are floribundas, which came to us around the turn of the century from Denmark.

Breeders are getting ever closer to creating the perfect easy-care shrub rose: one that blooms profusely and repeatedly, resists fungal diseases, has an attractive habit and abundant foliage and a glorious fragrance to boot.

honors for the first American shrub rose to pick up an award in Europe—the orchid pink groundcover 'Magic Carpet'.

Ralph Moore, the innovative "king of miniatures," dabbles in all sorts of roses, mixing old bloodlines with new. There will be many new striped roses coming onto the market soon, all from Ralph's original work with stripes. But he's gotten attention in the shrub world with two new rugosa hybrids, the soft yellow 'Topaz Jewel', and 'Linda Campbell', a cluster-flowered bright red. Watch for the first rugosa miniatures and modern crested moss hybrids.

Yellow shrub roses are still the most rare. Weeks Roses will be bringing out a variety, 'Flutterbye', which traces back to *Rosa soulieana* in its heritage. Clusters of single yellow flowers change color with each passing day on this beauty with glossy foliage.

# SUPPLIERS

While many of the modern roses recommended in this handbook are likely to be available in your local nursery, old roses aren't widely available. Here are some mail-order sources for old garden roses:

**ANTIQUE ROSE EMPORIUM**
Route 5, Box 143
Brenham, TX 77833
800-441-0002
Catalog, $5.00

**HORTICO, INC.**
723 Robson Rd., RR 1
Waterdown, Ontario L0R 2H1
Canada (no import restrictions)
905-689-6984
Catalog, $3.00

**BUTNER'S OLD MILL NURSERY**
806 South Belt Highway
St. Joseph, MO 64507
816-279-7434
Free catalog

**PICKERING NURSERIES**
670 Kingston Rd.
Pickering, Ontario L1V 1A6
Canada (no import restrictions)
905-839-2111
Catalog, $3.00

**HEIRLOOM OLD GARDEN ROSES**
24062 NE Riverside Drive
St. Paul, OR 97137
503-538-1576
Catalog, $5.00

**VINTAGE GARDENS**
2227 Gravenstein Highway So.
Sebastopol, CA 95472
707-829-2035
Catalog, $4.00

**HERITAGE ROSE GARDENS**
16831 Mitchell Creek Drive
Fort Bragg, CA 95437
707-964-3748
Catalog, $1.50

# RECOMMENDED READING

Beales, Peter. *Roses.* New York: Holt, 1992

*Combined Rose List 1994.* Compiled and edited by Peter Schneider. Rocky River, Ohio: Peter Schneider, 1994

Ellwanger, Henry Brooks. *The Rose.* New York: Dodd, Mead & Co., 1882

Harkness, Jack. *Roses.* London: Dent, 1978

Paul, William. *The Rose Garden.* London, 1848

Prince, William Robert. *A Treatise on Fruit and Ornamental Trees and Plants, Cultivated at the Linnaean Botanic Garden.* New York, 1820

Scanniello, Stephen, and Tania Bayard. *Roses of America: The Brooklyn Botanic Garden's Guide to Our National Flower.* New York: Henry Holt, 1990

Scanniello, Stephen, and Tania Bayard. *Climbing Roses.* New York: Prentice Hall(Macmillan)/Horticulture, 1994

Stevens, Glendon A. *Climbing Roses.* New York: Macmillan, 1933

Thomas, Graham Stuart. *Climbing Roses Old and New.* New York: St. Martin's Press, 1966

Wilson, Helen Van Pelt. *Climbing Roses.* New York: M. Barrows, 1955

❀

For more information on old garden roses, write:

Heritage Rose Foundation
1512 Gorman Street
Raleigh, NC 27606

# CONTRIBUTORS

JOHN AND MARIE BUTLER are amateur gardeners and old-rose enthusiasts in Chesterfield, Viriginia.

TOM CARRUTH is the hybridizer for Weeks Wholesale Rose Grower in Upland, California. He has worked in rose research for more than 18 years. Some of his roses include 'Crystalline', 'Fire 'n' Ice', 'Origami', 'Columbus', 'Heartbreaker' and 'Flutterbye'.

WILLENE CLARK is professor of art history at Marlboro College in Vermont, specializing in medieval and Victorian art. She grows roses and perennials around her mountainside home.

JOHN CLEMENTS is owner of Heirloom Old Garden Roses in St. Paul, Oregon, where he plants 40,000 rose seeds each year with an emphasis on breeding shrub and old garden roses. He has been growing roses commercially for 24 years, including old garden roses, and David Austin English Roses for the past eight years.

JOYCE DEMITS began collecting old garden roses and "lost roses" in Mendocino County and elsewhere in northern California 30 years ago. She is a member of the Heritage Rose Group, the Royal National Rose Society of Great Britain, and the Mendocino County Botanical Gardens.

LIZ DRUITT is a writer and gardener fascinated by historic plants and organic growing. She was Retail Garden Manager at the Antique Rose Emporium in Brenham, Texas, for three years, and co-authored the book, *Landscaping with Antique Roses* (1992, Taunton Press). Liz now operates her own garden consulting business, Creative Plots.

SUE FELDBAUM gardens in Brooklyn, New York, on a too small plot with too many roses.

KARL HOLMES is a horticultural consultant, garden designer and gardener. He is the former Rose Care Specialist at Harvard University's Arnold Arboretum.

JIM JOANNIDES has gardened in San Francisco and Los Angeles. He presently takes care of the rose plot at the Liz Christie Bowery Garden in New York City.

RICHARD A. KLINGENSMITH is a volunteer in the Cranford Rose Garden at the Brooklyn Botanic Garden. He raises roses, vegetables and berries in his backyard garden in Queens, New York.

# CONTRIBUTORS

RUTH KNOPF is a native of South Carolina who has collected and grown old roses for 18 years. She studies and photographs roses during her extensive travels in the U.S. and abroad.

GREGG LOWERY owns and operates Vintage Gardens, in Sebastopol, California, a retail and mail-order own-root rose nursery. He also grows more than 2,000 varieties of roses, both antique and modern, in his own collection.

DR. MALCOLM MANNERS is Associate Professor of Citrus and Ornamental Horticulture at Florida Southern College, where he manages a collection of more than 400 rose varieties and teaches courses in plant propagation. He is secretary and a trustee of the Heritage Rose Foundation and editor for the Central Florida Heritage Rose Society.

OZ AND AUDREY OSBORN are the past President and Secretary of the Garden State Rose Club of Tenafly, New Jersey. In addition to their six children, four grandchildren and two dogs, they enjoy their 350 rose bushes and going rose rustling throughout New Jersey.

PHILLIP ROBINSON has been an avid gardener since the age of eight, having learned his craft in the East Bay community of San Leandro, California. He is horticulturist at Korbel Champagne Cellars, where he restored the gardens surrounding the Korbel family summer home, the Korbel House. Today he coordinates all aspects of the landscape and gardens of Korbel.

STEPHEN SCANNIELLO is a world-renowned rosarian and curator of the Cranford Rose Garden in the Brooklyn Botanic Garden. He is co-author of *Roses of America* and *Climbing Roses,* and served as consultant and contributing author on several other horticultural books, among them the upcoming new edition of the Bush-Brown *America's Garden Book* and the recently released American Horticulture Society *Encyclopedia of Gardening.* He is chairperson for the Heritage Rose Foundation.

IDA SHARP is a native of Louisiana who is continuing her family tradition by growing roses both for pleasure and for commerce. Her specialty is antique roses, which she displays and grows at her cottage garden called Rose Hill Garden, north of Baton Rouge.

MIKE SHOUP owns and operates the Antique Rose Emporium in Brenham, Texas, a nursery devoted to the preservation and distribution of old garden roses.

# CONTRIBUTORS

TERI TILLMAN grows old roses, wildflowers and native plants around her restored 1840s home in Natchez, Mississippi.

CHARLES A. WALKER, JR. is president of the Heritage Rose Foundation. He has grown and studied heritage roses for more than 20 years.

# ILLUSTRATION CREDITS

Drawings by STEVE BUCHANAN.

Photos: Cover and pages 9 top left, top right and bottom left, 15, 19, 21, 23, 26, 27, 29, 31 top right and middle left, 33, 43, 47, 62 bottom, 63 right, 69 bottom, 70 top, 71 top, 77 right, 80 bottom, 81 left, 86 bottom, 87 top and bottom, 88 bottom, 89 top and bottom, 92 left and right, 93 left and right, 94 top, 95 left and right by STEPHEN SCANNIELLO.

Pages 1, 25, 81 right, 82 top by JERRY PAVIA.

Pages 5, 22, 24, 37 middle and right, 45, 56 right, 57 top and bottom, 58 top, 61 left, 62 top, 64 bottom, 65, 71 bottom, 74 top, 83 top by ALAN L. DETRICK.

Pages 9 bottom right, 40, 48, 63 left, 69 top, 97, 99 by JUDYWHITE.

Pages 11, 12 by RUTH KNOPF.

Pages 14, 41, 85 by GREGG LOWERY.

Page 31 top left, middle right, bottom left and bottom right by PAMELA HARPER.

Pages 34, 35 by VIRGINIA W. BROWN.

Pages 37 left, 55 top and bottom, 56 left, 61 right, 64 top, 68 bottom, 80 top, 83 bottom, 100 by CHRISTINE M. DOUGLAS.

Page 51 by MARIE AND JOHN BUTLER.

Pages 58 bottom, 68 top, 70 bottom, 73, 75 top and bottom, 76 top and bottom, 77 left, 82 bottom, 86 top, 88 top by MIKE SHOUP.

Page 74 bottom by IDA SHARP.

Page 79 by JOHN CLEMENTS.

Pages 91, 94 bottom by JIM JOANNIDES.

# HARDINESS ZONE MAP

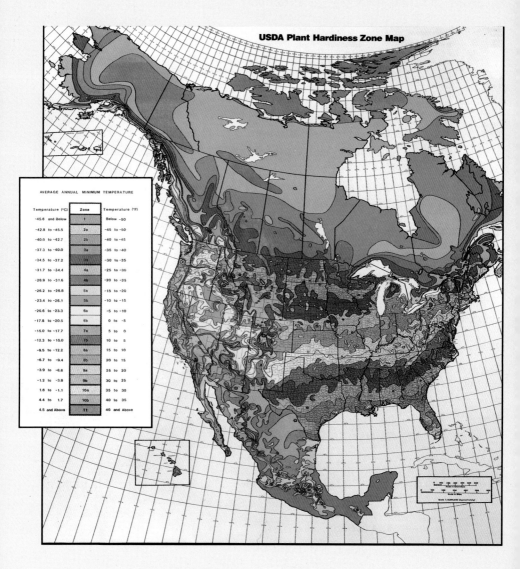

USDA Plant Hardiness Zone Map

AVERAGE ANNUAL MINIMUM TEMPERATURE

| Temperature (°C) | Zone | Temperature (°F) |
|---|---|---|
| -45.6 and Below | 1 | Below -50 |
| -42.8 to -45.5 | 2a | -45 to -50 |
| -40.0 to -42.7 | 2b | -40 to -45 |
| -37.3 to -40.0 | 3a | -35 to -40 |
| -34.5 to -37.2 | 3b | -30 to -35 |
| -31.7 to -34.4 | 4a | -25 to -30 |
| -28.9 to -31.6 | 4b | -20 to -25 |
| -26.2 to -28.8 | 5a | -15 to -20 |
| -23.4 to -26.1 | 5b | -10 to -15 |
| -20.6 to -23.3 | 6a | -5 to -10 |
| -17.8 to -20.5 | 6b | 0 to -5 |
| -15.0 to -17.7 | 7a | 5 to 0 |
| -12.3 to -15.0 | 7b | 10 to 5 |
| -9.5 to -12.2 | 8a | 15 to 10 |
| -6.7 to -9.4 | 8b | 20 to 15 |
| -3.9 to -6.6 | 9a | 25 to 20 |
| -1.2 to -3.8 | 9b | 30 to 25 |
| 1.6 to -1.1 | 10a | 35 to 30 |
| 4.4 to 1.7 | 10b | 40 to 35 |
| 4.5 and Above | 11 | 40 and Above |

# INDEX

# ❁ Gardening Books for the Next Century ❁ from the Brooklyn Botanic Garden

**Don't miss any of the gardening books in Brooklyn Botanic Garden's 21st-Century Gardening Series!** Published four times a year, these acclaimed books explore the frontiers of ecological gardening—offering practical, step-by-step tips on creating environmentally sensitive and beautiful gardens for the 1990s and the new century. Your subscription to BBG's 21st-Century Gardening Series is free with Brooklyn Botanic Garden membership.

**SUBSCRIPTIONS**

Please photocopy this form, complete and return to:
Brooklyn Botanic Garden, 1000 Washington Avenue, Brooklyn, NY 11225-1099.

Your name.............................................................................................................

Address................................................................................................................

City/State/Zip ........................................................Phone ..................................

AMOUNT

☐ Yes, I want to subscribe to the 21st-Century Gardening Series (4 quarterly volumes) by becoming a member of the Brooklyn Botanic Garden:

☐ $25 (Subscribing Member)     ☐ $125 (Supporting Member)

☐ $50 (Sustaining Member)     ☐ $300 (Contributing Member)    ..................

☐ Enclosed is my tax-deductible contribution to the Brooklyn Botanic Garden.    ..................

TOTAL    ..................

Form of payment: ☐ Check enclosed   ☐ Visa   ☐ Mastercard

Credit card# ...................................Exp ...............Signature ...............................

❁ For information on ordering any of the following back titles, please write the Brooklyn Botanic Garden at the above address or call (718) 622-4433, ext. 274.

American Cottage Gardening
Annuals: A Gardener's Guide
Bonsai: Special Techniques
Culinary Herbs
Dyes from Nature
The Environmental Gardener
Ferns
Garden Photography
The Gardener's World of Bulbs
Gardening for Fragrance
Gardening in the Shade
Gardening with Wildflowers
   & Native Plants

Going Native: Biodiversity
   in Our Own Backyards
Greenhouses & Garden Rooms
Herbs & Cooking
Herbs & Their Ornamental Uses
Hollies: A Gardener's Guide
Indoor Bonsai
Japanese Gardens
The Natural Lawn & Alternatives
Natural Insect Control
A New Look at Vegetables
A New Look at Houseplants

Orchids for the Home
   & Greenhouse
Ornamental Grasses
Perennials: A Gardener's Guide
Pruning Techniques
Roses
Shrubs: The New Glamour Plants
Soils
The Town & City Gardener
Trees: A Gardener's Guide
Water Gardening
The Winter Garden